Managing the Mental Game

How To Think More Effectively, Navigate Uncertainty, And Build Mental Fortitude

By

Jeff Boss

Leadership and Team Coach, Former Navy SEAL, and Author of *Navigating Chaos: How To Find Certainty In Uncertain Situations*

Dedication

To the fallen.
Gone but never forgotten.

This page intentionally left blank.

CONTENTS

OVERVIEW

This book is full of useful exercises gleaned from personal experience in managing pressure and stress amidst the most uncertain situations.

As a Navy SEAL, we were expected to find solutions to complex problems—without fail.

We operated on little guidance and even less information.

We comported ourselves in extremely stressful circumstances that would've caused many people to pee their pants (yup, I said it).

Despite the overwhelming stress, pressure and chaos of the moment, one of the defining characteristics that distinguished us from the enemy was this:

<u>We expected to win.</u>

No matter what threat the enemy posed or the danger of the moment, we *expected* to win.

Let me pose a question to you...

Do you *expect* to succeed?

Is "losing" so foreign to you that it doesn't even cross your mind?

If the answer is, "No" or "It depends" or "Not all the time," then this book is for you.

The materials in this book that I'm going to share with you are the exact tools that I used to overcome momentary overwhelm, and they will for you, too. Specifically, the insights into change and uncertainty provided in these pages along with the 23 exercises that build mental toughness are exactly what will propel you forward when others feel paralyzed.

Of course, there is a catch.

The exercises are only as good as the effort you put into internalizing the content and applying it. There is no magic death touch that will eliminate stress. After all, we are all human and emotion defines us. But if you work diligently to apply the lessons here, I guarantee *you* will be able to define your emotion, rather than being defined by it.

I put this guide together because more often than not, in my coaching practice I see similar mental challenges arise independent of industry:

- Fear of failure
- The need for control
- Fear of change
- Desire for greater personal fulfillment

The list goes on.

Thanks for purchasing this book. If you have any questions, comments or want to learn more, please visit http://www.chaosadvantage.com/

Okay, let's get started.

11 Takeaways You Will Get From This Book

1. Why understanding the mind is the smartest thing you can do

2. Learn the 4 mental traps and how to avoid them

3. The 3 types of focus and why mastering them is fundamental to success

4. Learn how to deal with uncertainty and not be stymied by fear

5. Learn the 3 pitfalls of uncertainty so you can anticipate and avoid them

6. The truth about managing uncertainty

7. Learn the neuroscience of change

8. Become proficient in replacing negative thoughts with positive ones

9. Create more productive thinking habits by understanding thought architecture

10. 23 exercises for navigating pressure

11. The secret to building mental fortitude

CHAPTER 1

LOBSTERS

In the center of an inkwell lobster pot is a steep hole that funnels a lobster into the bottom of the pot. The lobster cannot escape because the pot is designed to take advantage of the lobster's natural weaknesses: its physical characteristics and its behavior.

As a living organism, lobsters need food to survive, so bait is placed at the bottom of the pot to entice lobsters into crawling through the hole for their food. This is the first trap—the behavioral response.

The second trap takes advantage of the lobster's physicality to prevent him from escaping. The lobster cannot climb out because his claws won't allow it. His back is hard-shelled which means it can't contort and his claws prevent him from grasping anything.

This is the second trap: his physical characteristics.

What's the point of this example? The point is this.

Lobsters get trapped by being lobsters.

Who they are is exactly what traps them. It's their responses to the bait that derail and ultimately sink their survival. And you know what? Humans are no different.

Now, not all "bait" leads to binding situations, and some things about our physical makeup are just out of our control. However, our reactions to that bait certainly are within our control. More specifically, they're *chosen*.

> "One's philosophy is not best expressed in words; it is expressed in the choices one makes... and the choices we make are ultimately our responsibility." - Eleanor Roosevelt

It has been said before and it's worth saying again:

Change is constant, but progress isn't.

To deal with the inevitable Murphy Factor that likes to arise at the most inopportune times to test our resolve, we need to be prepared to deal with anything.

Of course, being prepared for "anything" is quite a large undertaking. In fact, it's not exactly possible to be prepared *for* anything. But what is possible is being prepared to *respond* to "anything," and that begins with ourselves.

Managing the mental game is about harnessing your ability to focus, visualize, set goals and talk effectively to yourself; it's about mastering the art of effortlessness that defines elite athletes, top businesspeople, and other top tier performers.

Let's consider, for a moment, elite performers.

Elite performers—in both sport and in business—thrive amidst uncertainty. They perform despite—not because of—the pressure. Their success is the result of detailed planning, not to mention the following:

Visualization. Visualizing what success looks like such that their brains only have to go through the motions.

Goal-setting. Setting and hitting hundreds of small goals that subsequently lead to one massive achievement.

Smart thinking. Positive self-talk encourages and explores intention rather than limits them—and intention is the precursor to actionable behavior.

Elite performers use competition as a means to hone their skills, to continually reinvent the value they bring to the table (or the field), to stay relevant, and to remain ahead of the curve.

However, they do so through constant and deliberate practice such that by the time they reach "game time," which may be a sales opportunity, business deal, or competitive sporting event, they no longer have to think. Instead, they just act.

Constant practice allows you to shorten the gap between stimulus and response such that the thinking that connects "A" to "B" becomes faster, thus driving a quicker reaction time.

When we enter into a new industry, adopt a new skill, assume a new hobby, there's a learning curve that slowly winds upward through four stages of learning:

Unconscious Incompetence

This is the "I-don't-know-that-I-don't-know-how-to-do-this" stage. This is the only time when it's okay to be ignorant (that's a joke).

Conscious Incompetence

This is the most difficult of the four stages for a couple reasons. First, it can be overwhelming to realize there's a gap between where you are and where you want to be, followed by the realization of what it takes to fill that gap. This is what Peter Senge refers to in his book The Fifth Discipline as emotional tension—the feelings of overwhelm, despair, and anxiety that we associate with just how much effort is needed to get to the place where we want to be.

Second, humans naturally impose judgment. We pass judgment about ourselves and others that may or may not be true but, without confirmation of those judgments, we believe them regardless. This is a dangerous place to be when assessing your own progress because it can quickly lead down the road of self-defeating beliefs. But when you push past the negativity in this stage, you're halfway there.

Conscious Competence

Being consciously competent means you're aware of your newfound skills but they're not automatic yet. There's still a degree of, well, conscious effort applied to learning. In this stage is also where you see defensive behavior.

Unconscious Competence

Think *ninja*. To be unconsciously competent means you're not even aware of the impact or skill you bring because it's already a part of you; it's ingrained into who you are and what you do. Here's a quick storyboard example to highlight each of the four stages of learning:

You just turned 16 and want to obtain your driver's license. At first you think that driving on the road will be easy. After all, the only thing you have to do is spin that big wheel and press on the pedal, right? This is unconscious incompetence—the stage where you don't know what you don't know yet, and in this case, you don't know about stopping distance, slick or ice covered roads, reaction times, road rage or incredibly slow drivers.

But, once you sign up for a driver education class—which is roughly five days of your life that you'll never get back—you begin to learn about everything you didn't realize before. You raise your level of learning to conscious incompetence because now you're aware of all those "things" you don't actually know.

You begin practicing your three-point turns, parallel parking, and driving in reverse. But, there are steps you go through in your mind to recall each one so you can execute them effectively:

- Get parallel to the car ahead of you before you attempt to parallel park.
- Look over your shoulder so you can see better.
- Be aware of everything around your car and try not to hit them.

After a while, you no longer have to think through each step because you've performed this maneuver enough. In other words, you've graduated from conscious competence to unconscious competence.

Apply the same learning to the exercises and principles in this book and your learning will skyrocket. Guaranteed.

What To Expect From This Book

Nothing. Don't expect anything. The moment you expect rapid change or immediate success to *simply occur* is the moment you let yourself down and submit a one star review of this book.

Why? Because nothing good ever comes without effort. It takes hard work to rewire your brain and reverse years of habitual thinking into another, more effective, way.

When I said above not to expect anything, what I meant was that the takeaways and applications from this book are only as good as the effort you put forth to learn and apply them. Nothing good ever comes easily (well, most things), and teaching yourself better self-management under pressure can only be tested in one of two ways:

1) During an actual pressure moment
2) During a simulated pressure moment

The latter is preferable simply because it's training, as there are no real implications if you don't get the "right answer." Unfortunately, the resources available at our disposal to leverage such opportunities (i.e. coaches, mentors, time, money) are limited.

What does this mean for you?

It means that your own self-awareness and willingness to track and measure your progress play an even greater role in helping you achieve your goals. If you're a lone ranger going about this process of redefining yourself or simply learning to expand the tools at your disposal to relate with change and uncertainty, there are a few individually-led measures you can take to ensure you stay on track. Personal application is fundamental for the same reason that you can't lead others until you can lead yourself.

Focus On Fundamentals

In the SEAL Teams, we didn't progress to the next level of training until each member grasped not only a basic understanding of the fundamentals but could also demonstrate them under duress. After all, if you can put four to five bullets in the hole the size of a quarter under the pressure of time and competition, chances are you already have the fundamentals pretty well established.

The same is true for effective thinking, managing stress and dealing with uncertainty.

Random Exercise

Keep a notecard with you. Every time you feel stress from someone or something, write it down. Be sure to annotate:

- The source of stress
-The thought(s) that ran through your mind upon becoming aware of the stressor (this is noticing your self-talk—what you say to yourself in the moment. More on this later.)
-The environment (people involved, personality types, formal/informal setting...)

Don't get too crazy with details—you don't want to dissuade yourself from tracking your goals. Just keep track of how many times throughout the day and why you felt stressed.

There are fundamentals for learning how to structure your thoughts more effectively that you will learn in this book. Just as you learn how to outline a research paper in school, dealing with the pressure and stress of the moment requires the same *fundamental* application. It's a deliberate process.

You can't deal with chaos until you know how to deal with yourself. This book will show you how.

"In chaos there is opportunity." - Sun Tzu

CHAPTER 2

4 MENTAL TRAPS AND HOW TO AVOID THEM

Human thinking is setup for traps. Actually, we're wired to be *vulnerable* to traps, but through awareness and deliberate practice we can better manager our reactions amidst uncertain situations and improve our likelihood of success. Success, in this context, is defined as:

- greater self-control
- stronger focus
- better decision-making
- effective thinking
- healthier habits

By changing our thinking about a particular trap—specifically, when we identify 1) the existence of a trap and 2) your reaction to it—we can more effectively and efficiently bridge the gap between where we are and where we want to be. Here's a quick diagram to illustrate the types of mental traps we all experience at one point or another:

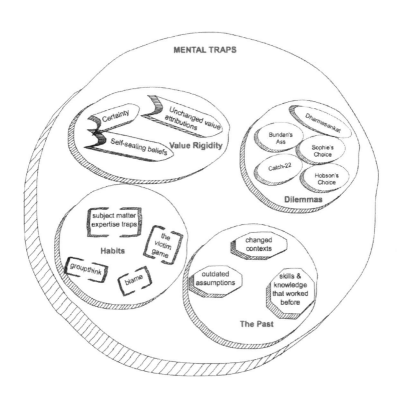

Let's go through each of the above four traps and see how they affect our thinking.

The Past Traps

Have you ever heard something like, "we've always done X this way so why should we change it?" The past is a trap; a trap of excuses *not* to change.

However, the problem is this. When we're immersed in our own environments we become products of those environments—a dangerous place where groupthink, confirmation and availability bias co-exist.

This may sound obvious, but it isn't. Remember that confirmation bias is the tendency to search for, interpret, favor, and recall information in a way that confirms your own beliefs or hypotheses, while giving disproportionately less consideration to other possibilities.

Availability bias is a mental shortcut that relies on immediate examples that come to mind when evaluating a specific topic, concept, method or decision. Let's look at the following example.

Company XYZ is a $10 billion company. Certain vice presidents have been there for 17, 18, and even 20 plus years and they claim that they still do the same things today—perform the same behaviors, execute the same mantras—as they did 10 or 15 years ago.

I call bullshit. Here's why.

What it takes to move a company from $1 billion to $5 billion to $10 billion are all very different things. Moreover, unless you were hired as a vice president from day one and have spent 17 plus years in that role, chances are you've adopted new management and leadership practices to stay competitive.

However, since this particular executive is *still* with the company and has been successful, it's easy to attribute his success to the past because that's what got him to his current position.

The past is a trap unless we learn from it. When we learn from past mistakes then the past becomes an incredibly valuable learning opportunity; when we rely on the past to predict the future then we become complacent, and it's not soon after complacency arrives that chaos occurs. If you want a real-life example of a business who became complacent, just look up Blockbuster, Encyclopedia Britannica, KB Toys, Napster, or any of the other organizations that failed to adapt because they failed to question the status quo.

Why? Because it's easier to make decisions based upon what we already know than try to anticipate what we don't, or what *could* be. It's also more comforting to make *easier* decisions—ones that require little effort—than difficult ones. Just think of that problematic colleague you worked with in the past and how having a conversation with that person wasn't going to be easy. The majority of people would avoid having that conversation and hope that the problem self-corrects, because it's easier to think that way.

Anyway, the anticipation of change bedevils our decision-making because *anticipation* itself is illusory.

Habit Traps

While more on habits will be discussed later in this book, I want to touch on how habits play a significant role in trapping us mentally.

When you think of a habit, what comes to mind? An automatic behavior? An immediate reaction? What this infers is that when the gap between stimulus and response is too short (i.e. when you react too quickly) then judgment and decision-making diminish to the point that consequences become blurry, rendering you incapable of seeing alternatives. This is what happens when we're accused of being "too quick to judge" or "overly critical."

The Victim Game

Believing you're a victim is an easy trap to fall into because, after all, *we're* never wrong; it's always someone else, right?

Wrong.

Playing the "victim game" is a self-perpetuating mental trap that hides reasonable options, discourages us from finding better ones, and gnaws away at our desire to improve the situation.

How do you avoid playing the "victim game?" Easy. You choose not to play. It's that simple.

Blame

Blame is dead-end thinking because it doesn't take you anywhere except to victimhood; if playing victim is the destination, then blame is the highway that leads there. Why? Well, aside from the negativity associated with blame (it avoids personal responsibility and accountability), the nature of blame ends in an absolute which closes any avenues to improving the situation.

For instance, if Sara blames Mike, saying, "Mike is just stupid. There's no way around it" then Sara has shutdown any and all avenues of trying to improve Mike's stupidity. Don't get me wrong, there are definitely stupid people out there and I've come across quite a bit of them—I've even been one from time to time—but that doesn't mean they'll never be smart (just that they're not smart right now).

How do you avoid blame? Approach your next "blame situation" from the perspective that "Mike" (or whomever) is doing what he believes to be the right and the best way to do X. If his definition of success differs from yours, then that's a great opportunity for a conversation.

Subject Matter Expertise

If you're a hammer, then everything tends to look like a nail.

I'm guilty of this mindset myself. When someone presents a problem to me I immediately want to solve it because that's my nature.

However, there are two problems with this mindset:

1) Blaming my response on my nature is to blame (and we already discussed that)
2) Not everything falls within my (or anybody's) subject matter expertise

It's easy to get trapped doing what you're already good at and to lead yourself into thinking that, since you solved problem A, then problems B, C, and D are equally solvable using the same methods.

Dilemma Traps

A dilemma is a decision with two ugly options. *Burden's Ass* illustrates the paradox of free will. A donkey is stuck midway between two options: a pile of hay to his left, and a bucket of water to his right. He's both hungry and thirsty and simply cannot choose which one to try first. So he dies.

Dharmasankat is a Sanskrit word that infers a moral dilemma, or "troubled duty." One example is the dilemma imposed upon world leaders to either protect innocent people from terror, or attack the attackers and risk collateral damage.

Hobson's choice isn't really a choice but a take-it-or-leave-it dilemma—both of which are less than ideal.

Value Rigidity Traps

Have you ever been water skiing and, as the skier, wanted to hold on to the line *after* having fallen, such that you're being dragged across the water on your stomach rather than on your skis?

Or, how about the unfortunate house fire? Upon discovering your house is on fire, you run out of the house only to remember that precious Pooky the cat is still inside, just waiting to be incinerated. You go back inside to retrieve Pooks but the roof collapses, sealing both of your fates.

I know. This is a bit morbid of an example but this is value rigidity: when you refuse to reappraise what's important to you. Not to say that your feline isn't important, but weighed against the larger value of your own life, where do you draw the line?

Although this is an extreme example, it highlights the fact that changing circumstances necessitate changing perspectives, and one of the way in which we perceive the outer world stems from our values.

How To Escape A Mental Trap

It's easy to say, "the best way to avoid a trap is to never put oneself in that position in the first place" but this neglects the very definition *of* mental traps: unconscious biases that exist below our level of awareness.

There is no prevention to falling into a trap. It happens. But, there is certainly a way to minimize the amount of time one spends in that trap, and that begins with creating awareness.

Creating awareness by oneself isn't easy. Doing so would be akin to what Einstein said, "You cannot solve a problem through the same thinking that got you there." Moreover, I would be out of a job as an executive coach.

What you can do, however, is build your mental repertoire to manage yourself when those traps occur, and that's what this book is about.

Chapter 3

3 TYPES OF FOCUS (AND WHY MASTERING THEM IS FUNDAMENTAL TO SUCCESS)

Focus is a function of the brain, and since the brain is a muscle, that means focus is, too. What's important to note here is that focus can be exercised, strengthened and improved, much like it can wither away into weakness without a concerted effort (or focus) to improve it.

3 Types of Focus[1]

There are three ways in which we focus: internal, external, and people. Internal focus entails just

[1] The Focal C model may have had sections of focus actually highlights a fourth type of focus

that—directing attention toward our own personal values, intuitions, and decision-making. People focus places relationships at the forefront of our attention; external focus determines how all the above relate to each other and fit within a larger system.

The challenge with focus is combating its evil nemesis known as *distractions*. If it weren't for distractions, then we would all have the laser-like focus every ninja-wannabe espouses. But we don't. And it's because distractions get the better of us. Rather, we *let* distractions get the better of us because our focus isn't strong enough to tell our distractions to just "go away!" So, we must build it.

At the center of these three types of focus is where we find balance. After all, if our focus weighs more heavily in one area, then other areas will suffer. If, for instance, your focus is geared too heavily inward then you become oblivious to your external environment and the people around you. If you focus too heavily on others then time for yourself suffers. The key is managing distractions such that our internal, external, and people areas of focus are optimized at the right moment.

Much like applying the right leadership style for the right personality or situation, Daniel Goleman, psychologist and bestselling author, identifies two main types of distractions: sensory and emotional. **Sensory distractions** are easily ignored. You're probably not paying attention to the blank margins as you read this text, or noticing how your tongue rests firmly against the roof of your mouth.

What's more disruptive are the **emotional distractions**, such as a shaky relationship that went awry or unfavorable social judgment that keeps invading our thoughts.

While the intent of these distractions isn't necessarily bad (to find resolution), the cycle of rumination into which we fall certainly is. This is why people fall into a "funk" and can't get out of it. Their brains are replaying the emotional distraction over and over to try to make sense of it to no avail. It's a self-perpetuating—and self-defeating—cycle of worry. As a wise, green-little creature once said, "Your focus is your reality" – Yoda.

Why Uncertainty Is Paralyzing

Facing your fears is one of the most courageous things anybody can do. The personal willingness to look uncertainty in the eye, slap it across the face and say, "You don't scare me" is admirable to say the least.

And best of all, it **can be learned**.

You don't remain at the tip of the spear if you don't like the wind in your face. It's not natural to enjoy—much less, love—pressure. To do so, however, you have to first make a conscious choice to devote yourself passionately to self-improvement.

Greg Searle, Olympic rowing gold medalist, is often asked whether success was worth the price he paid for the sacrifices he made. His answer: "I never made any sacrifices; I made choices." (See the chapter on **thought architecture** for how to do this), and he did so because he knew what he wanted.

Self-limiting beliefs—fear—is the barrier between you and your authentic self; between who you are and the person you want to be.

Fear of the unknown stems from within. You may have little exposure—and therefore competence—in dealing with it (whatever "it" is) and so the thought of learning how to do so is simply too much at the moment. We don't fear learning; we just don't associate the process of learning with anything inside our comfort zones. Instead, we often avoid change because of the inconvenience associated with learning something new.

Nerd Alert[2]

Xenophobia is derived from the Greek word "Xenos," meaning "foreigner or stranger," and Phobos, which means "morbid fear.

When uncertainty presents itself, we experience discomfort in a number of different physiological ways:

- Sweaty palms and/or forehead
- Increased heart rate
- Shallow breathing

[2] There will be random "nerd alerts" throughout the book—good facts to know.

- Dilated pupils (the brain wants to absorb as much information as possible, so in an effort to do so, it tells the eyes to "get big!")
- Shaking, trembling
- Wet pants (that's a joke)

To remedy the physiological effects of pressure, you need to know two things:

1) What uncertainty may arise
2) How you <u>will</u> deal with it

I underlined <u>will</u> because change (read *uncertainty*) happens fast, and it's not a question of whether you will deal with it or not—since *not* dealing with change is still dealing with it—but a question of *how* you will face it. Let's look at the types of uncertainty that can arise and the traps of each.

<u>Pitfalls of Uncertainty</u>

There are three pitfalls that characterize uncertainty:

Pitfall #1: Uncertainty is Boundless

The unknown manifests itself everywhere—in traffic, at the office, in school, at home. And because the prospect for uncertainty exists *everywhere* then so too does the element of fear, which means the potential to get caught up in the moment, freeze, and perform *less* than ideal is always there, too.

Pitfall #2: Uncertainty is Hidden

If we knew when uncertainty was going to poke its ugly little head out then we would feel more control in the moment and less fear. But we don't, because uncertainty appears at any moment, unannounced and unwelcome, and presents a choice for us either to face it head on, or find a road *more* traveled (read *easier*).

Pitfall #3: Uncertainty is Unhealthy if Unmanaged

The pressure of the moment, the stress buildup of worry leads to not just more gray hair but all the negative effects of stress we all know about, such as high blood pressure, headaches, depression, anxiety, etc…

Here's the good news: Knowing what these pitfalls cause is the first step to combatting them. You can't solve a problem without first identifying what the problem is. Moreover, you don't want to problem-solve the wrong solution. Surely this concept is intuitive, but its application isn't.

Here's what I mean.

3 Fallacies Of Managing Change That You Thought Worked (But Really Don't)

Even though your intentions to help a friend or family member navigate uncertainty are positive, you may just be providing fuel to the fire. The means by which you support and enable behavior in others may actually be detrimental. Below are three commonly used remedies people use to support others that *don't* work:

Bad Remedy #1: Offering Support

I know. It's completely counterintuitive but hear me out. Support can actually magnify stress and decrease performance on skill-based tasks simply because self-consciousness about success grows, so your focus moves away from "execute" mode and into "oh-my-gosh-what-are-they-thinking-of-me" mode.

In other words, a rise in self-focus disrupts the procedural knowledge of execution that the brain knows how to do, but doesn't because now the focus has changed. This is especially true if you have a greater need for acceptance or approval by others. The fear in this case isn't that you'll let people down, it's that they'll reject you if you fail.

Bad Remedy #2: Incentivizing

In Daniel Pink's book Drive: The Surprising Truth About What Motivates Us, he cites purpose, mastery, and autonomy as three drivers of motivation that replace the old carrot and stick approach of dangling money in front of an employee.

The challenge with tangible incentives is this: They increase the pressure of the moment (because there's seemingly more at stake) and cause a shift of focus from the task at hand to the consequences of failing at that task. The mental horsepower needed to problem solve is now being used to weigh out the possible gain or loss of the incentive (more on the benefit of focusing on process over task later). As a result, you give the problem less than your undivided attention—and effort.

Consider the following in the context of incentivizing yourself and others:

Listen to your language. Do you use phrases such as "I need…" or "I must…?" If so, you may be creating greater stress for yourself than necessary.

Using words that connote an all-or-nothing outcome does two things. First, it creates a sense of top-down pressure to perform, as if the demand to do [task] is coming from the external (but it's not, it's coming from you). In doing so, you create undue pressure upon yourself to execute the task. Instead, replace those words of an involuntary nature with words that connote something voluntary, such as, "I *choose* to…," or "I want to…".

Distinguish your needs from wants. There's a difference between *needing* a new pair of shoes and *wanting* them. If you didn't get the shoes, would you still survive? Yes, of course. So, that's a want—you *want* that new pair because they'll make you run faster (well, that's what the commercial said at least so it <u>must</u> be true, right?). However, you don't necessarily *need* more shoes because chances are you A) already have some and B) will still be able to live without them.

Nerd Alert #2

Needs are necessary for survival; wants make surviving fun.

Bad Remedy #3: Competing

I'm not saying that competition is bad. I am a firm believer in the value of competition and the competitive spirit. Rather, what's important to take away here is the perception of competition and how viewing it in a certain way can act as a pitfall of uncertainty that grows larger and larger if unmanaged, thus leading to decreased performance.

Here's what I mean.

If you view competition as a defining characteristic of your being, your self-worth and your image, you've now adopted a self-defeating belief. Those who view everything as a contest and feel they must win no matter what because anything less would make them look bad are driven by insecurity as they constantly feel the need to prove themselves in everything they do.

Not good.

Conversely, those who see failure as an opportunity to learn from, grow, and apply toward the *effort* of winning next time, don't get bogged down when uncertainties arise; they see tension and ambiguity as temporary lapses in time that are neither helpful nor hindering—they just <u>exist</u>.

Those Who See Failure As...	
"Final"...	**"Temporary"...**
Tend to give up easily when confronted with obstacles	Persist because each "failure" is a lesson learned
May see effort as intrinsic and un-developable	See effort as the path to mastery
Become defensive when receiving feedback	Embrace feedback as learning opportunities
View the success of others as a personal threat	Gain inspiration and learn from the success of others

CHAPTER 4

THE TRUTH ABOUT MANAGING UNCERTAINTY

The truth is that when **uncertainty** arises it is often accompanied by pressure, stress, and general physiological discomfort (some might even say "queasiness"), and although we can't control the stimulus of those stressors and pressures, we can control our responses to them.

Try this. Select any/all of the following circumstances that most resonate with you:

☐ You often justify bad habits by convincing yourself that they're "not *really* that bad."

☐ You experience anxiety when there are changes in your routine.

☐ You worry that making any changes in an already bad situation will make things even worse.

☐ You find it difficult to sustain change even after making a concerted effort.

☐ It's difficult to adapt to changes made by family, friends, or employees.

☐ You worry that any changes you make will only last for the short-term.

☐ The thought of stepping outside your comfort zone makes you feel uncomfortable.

☐ You lack the motivation to create positive change because you think doing so is too hard.

☐ You make excuses for why you can't change, such as "I'd like to exercise more, but my spouse doesn't want to go with me."

In her book 13 Things Mentally Strong People Don't Do: Take Back Your Power, Embrace Change, Face Your Fears, and Train Your Brain for Happiness and Success, author Amy Morin cites how "choosing to do something different requires you to adapt your thinking and your behavior" which naturally lead to negative emotions.

Nerd Alert #3
Response vs. Reaction

A **reaction** is involuntary. It's what happens when you touch your finger to a hot burner on the stove; it's a <u>re</u>-action.

A **response** is voluntary; it's <u>pro</u>-active in nature because it's chosen.

For example, in between stimulus and response there's a gap; a temporary pause that affords you the opportunity to *choose* how you'll respond. The difference between those who enjoy public speaking, for example, and those that don't is how they see the problem. People who enjoy speaking before audiences *choose* to see it as an opportunity to grow, to market oneself, to overcome a fear, whereas those who avoid the stage *choose* to see it as a forum for social judgment—namely, negative judgment toward themselves.

Chaos—and the uncertainty associated with chaos—cannot be controlled. Chaos can, however, be corralled. Let me explain.

The very nature of change—of the "unpredictable"—prevents us from assigning a clear-cut strategy to dealing with it effectively, since you can't assign a solution to a problem that doesn't yet exist or is ill-defined. What you can do is coordinate your behavioral responses *to* chaos such that uncertainty has no chance of survival when it tries to overtake you, and to do so requires two things:

1) **Self-awareness.** You must first know how you respond if you want to "course correct" your behavior.

2) **Self-management.** Once you're aware you can now tailor how you'll respond. Yes, this is difficult and yes, this requires willpower, focus, unlearning old habits for newer, healthier ones.

How do you manage yourself better? That's what we'll explore later in this book. For now, let's consider **two truths about uncertainty.**

First, the pressure of the moment disrupts what we value most, such as our relationships, careers, effectiveness as a parent, and our core ethical and moral decision-making.

The consequences of pressure can break a marriage, derail a career, and cause children to pull away from their parents or feel the need to cheat to meet their parents' expectations, all which compromise your integrity.

Second, people who handle pressure better than others do not "rise to the occasion" or perform statistically better than they do in non-pressure situations, they just manage themselves better.

In the SEAL Teams, for instance, we had a saying that "you don't rise to the occasion; you fall to the level of your training." There is no such thing as time management, only self-management.

Uncertainty is no different.

CHAPTER 5

THE

NEUROSCIENCE OF
CHANGE

"Man is not troubled by events but rather how he interprets them." - Epictetus

Have you ever wondered why some people just don't get ruffled while others run around as if their hair was on fire?

According to a study of 268 executives, presence is a deciding factor when it comes to promotion, and if your ability to self-manage is akin to a ticking time bomb, then your promotion potential is limited.

Leaders who speak well in front of audiences, maintain composure, and command a room appear to be calm, cool and collected—a quality mere mortals seek to emulate, rather than the typical fight, flight, or freeze response that they let overtake them in moments of high stress or pressure.

A Quick Lesson In Neurobiology

The fight, flight, or freeze response occurs when we perceive a threat—something that threatens our physical, mental, emotional or spiritual well-being. It could be something as mundane as being called a "chicken" like Marty McFly (played by Michael J. Fox) in the movie Back To The Future, or something more aggressive such as an angry debate or physical assault.

When the perception is made that danger is imminent, a message is sent to your brain's amygdala telling it to "watch out!" Consequently, the amygdala responds by telling the brain to secrete hormones to tell the nervous system to "get ready!" As a result, your palms sweat, shallow breathing ensues, and your peripheral vision narrows. To ease the burden of this overabundance of emotion you (perhaps subconsciously) choose to fight, flight, or freeze.

However, since neither fighting nor fleeing are ideal in a business setting (I can think of reasons why freezing before making a decision is important), you don't get a release. Instead, that bucket of emotion keeps filling up while your mind is saying, "Wait! Stop! I don't know how to process this!" The result is a "freak out" moment or temper tantrum because the brain and body are caught in an unbreakable feedback loop—much like married couple who bicker, debate and argue but don't really *hear* what the other person is saying.

Here's a more scientific explanation.

In the book Performing Under Pressure: The Science Of Doing Your Best When It Matters Most, the authors cite John Coates of Cambridge University and the discoveries he's made conducting studies on the effects of uncertainty and cortisol on behavior. From the book:

"John spent a decade on Wall Street, first trading independently and later managing derivative trading desks at Goldman Sachs and Deutsche Bank in the 2000s. After a decade in the financial world, John decided to leave finance to study neuroscience at Cambridge University. John and his team hypothesized that the physiological arousal that traders experienced when facing uncertainty and pressure had a profound effect on their trading decisions, particularly in market bubbles and crashes. He believed that their physiology systematically changed traders' risk preferences. In other words, they were taking too much risk in bull markets (when the market was going up) and not enough risk in bear markets (when the market was going down).

So the Cambridge team set up a series of experiments in The City, London's equivalent to Wall Street, to test their hypothesis, collecting a range of traders' biological markers over the course of their day and in various markets.

They found that in bear or down markets, traders' cortisol levels went up to such an extent that it led to risk aversion and an irrational focus on negative information in their environment. Cortisol is an important hormone when it comes to how we react under pressure. Principal among them is its effect on our ability to think and to retrieve memory. Along with another chemical, corticotrophin-releasing hormone (CRH), produced by the amygdala, cortisol incites anxiety, commonly called "anticipatory anxiety," and suppresses the production of testosterone. Testosterone acts to invigorate behavior. In the absence of testosterone, approach-based behavior diminishes and our attention becomes selectively focused on the negative aspects of a situation. Called attentional bias, it causes us to see all the stimuli in our environment as threatening. We become more paranoid. We amplify the negative. In effect, Coates found that the uncertainty that traders faced sharply increased their cortisol, and caused feelings of anxiety and fear."

Here's The Takeaway

Advances in neuroscience reveal that remaining calm under pressure isn't just an inborn trait but rather a skill that can be learned and developed. If it weren't, then I would've had to come up with a new concept for a book. The fact is, too little and/or too much stimulation leads to derailed or foggy thinking, poor impulse control, sub-par memory, ineffective decision-making, and a lack of empathy. Empathy is important because it allows you to *understand* others' points of view. Empathy and sympathy aren't the same. Empathy is placing yourself in the other person's shoes to see what they see and experience what they experience so you can better relate, and relationships drive business. Sympathy, however, is feeling *for* them. You find empathy by listening to the other person and not thinking about what to say next. You find sympathy in the dictionary between "shit" and "syphilis." Just sayin'.

Chapter 6

Learn to Replace Negative Thoughts With Positive Ones

We all have them: those seemingly "innocent" little thoughts that don't appear to have much weight but add up to costly emotional withdrawals.

What I'm referring to are those inconvenient intruders of negative self-talk that invade our personal space (i.e. our brains) and try to hold us back from doing something, limit our beliefs, or otherwise rationalize an abnormal idea into something acceptable.

Every time you hear that "other" voice tell you, "I can't do [this]," "that's too hard," or "I'm not good enough," you validate yourself—but not in a good way. The more often you send a negative message to your brain, the more often it believes that message to be true. It (the brain) doesn't have a choice; it can't tell the difference between reality and fiction, it just knows what you tell it.

You Are Your Thoughts

The mind is a powerful thing. It's both the problem and the solution to the challenges we face. By understanding how the mind works we gain a better understanding of what causes those challenges—as well as the solutions to overcoming them.

We live in a cause-effect world in terms of thought. In other words, for every action there's a reaction; for every cause, an effect. There are complements to every thought and every behavior we execute at any given moment.

To optimize ourselves, we need to understand the reactions and pro-actions of these complements because the accuracy of a particular thought, for example, determines the relevant accuracy of its behavioral consequence. This is a fifty-dollar way of saying <u>we get out what we put in.</u>

However, the challenge is this: we don't know what optimal looks like.

How do you know if your performance is ideal?

How do you know if you're working at your peak?

How can you tell if you're really pushing yourself or if it just *feels* like it?

The answer can be found in two types of thoughts.

2 Types of Thoughts You Need to Know

I can't remember where I heard this story before but it's good—it highlights the two aspects of thought that we use every day (and I'll explain each one afterward).

Fred was riding the subway one day during rush hour. Like every trip during the peak of pedestrian traffic, this subway car was jammed pack which precluded Fred from acquiring a seat. Tired after a long day, he just wanted to sit down. After all, an hour and a half subway commute is only fun if you've never traveled on the subway before (and even then it gets old after ten minutes).

Anyway, at the next stop the majority of passengers disembark which frees up some seats for Fred to sit.

Elated, he finally gets some much desired rest. But not for long.

Ten minutes later, the traffic picks up again and a swarm of people enter the subway car. Sitting to the right of the entry door, Fred notices a little old lady enter and head left, looking for a seat. He wonders who will get up and give their seat to the old lady and expects that the young man sitting and staring ahead will get up and move—especially since the surrounding passengers are female.

But, much to Fred's chivalrous dismay, the young man doesn't budge. Actually, he doesn't even look up to offer his seat to the old lady! Disappointed with the young man's lack of chivalry, the woman sitting next to the young man gets up and gives *her* seat to the old lady, turns back to the young man, scoffs, and turns away.

Fred is dumbfounded. He can't figure out why this young man didn't offer his seat, so he walked over and asked him, "Hey, didn't you see that old lady looking to sit down? Is chivalry *completely* dead?"

"Huh?" the young man is confused. "I'm sorry…I…didn't notice. I just learned I lost my father today and have been thinking about him ever since."

What We See And What We Know

The story above demonstrates the two types of thoughts that pervade our thinking, oftentimes without us even realizing it. **Relative thoughts** are those impressions that we perceive to be right. We perceive them as accurate because they're relative to how *we* would act. In the story above, Fred's relative thought was that the young man should've stood up and abdicated his seat to the old lady, because that's what Fred would've done. Fred's expectation for the young man was relative to the expectation he has of himself.

Conversely, **absolute thoughts** are those impressions that *are* accurate, such as the description of a word, an event, or a physical characteristic. Now, while both these thoughts *seem* disparate, they co-exist, and whenever there's coexistence there's the potential for one "reality" to bleed into the other; to obscure its complementary "reality" such that what we once believed to be true is now false, and vice versa.

I know, this is deep. In fact, I'm pretty sure I'm confusing myself right now (which isn't difficult to do, incidentally. That's a joke).

So, the question becomes, how do you stay in the bubble of absolute thought and mitigate the subjectivity of relative thought?

How To Manage Your Thoughts

Think for a moment, of the desert. Even if you've never been to the desert you know what it looks like. It's hot, dry, and lots of sand.

Now, think of the ocean. And even if you've never been to the ocean you know how to imagine it—a big body of water, right?

Congratulations, you just proved to yourself that you're capable of managing your own thoughts. This is the essence of building mental fortitude—accepting personal responsibility and accountability for the thoughts that enter your mind. A brief note on responsibility vs. accountability…

Responsibility: something is bestowed upon you; can be delegated.

Accountability: something for which you must answer; cannot be delegated.

Try this. For five days, pay attention to your thoughts and subsequent feelings and behaviors. Specifically, focus on the choices you make as a result of your thoughts. Notice whether they cause you to fight, flee, or freeze in the moment. If your thoughts aren't getting you the behavior you want, what are the complementary thoughts you want to have? How can you inject those thoughts into your mind and push the other ones out to get the results you want? What are the absolute and relative thoughts you might've had and how can they be better informed next?

Aside from the self-awareness this exercise creates, you'll also learn how your thoughts align with your vision, mission, and/or purpose and how they act as early warning signs of (un)desirable behavior.

A 10 Step Guide To Shaping Your Intention

Here are ten principles for shaping a positive intention:

1. Position it from the positive.

2. Stay active. (use present tense).

3. Elevate your intention to "optimal."

4. Focus on the now (focus on *being* rather than *doing*).

5. Affirm your intention.

6. Experience your intention (contrast is the divergence between physical, emotional and spiritual experiences).

7. Log it. An unwritten goal is a dream. Additionally, writing serves as another experiential component.

8. Read it.

9. Remember it. What did you notice when you read it aloud? What feelings passed through your body? What senses peaked? What words would you use to describe how your intention felt as you *heard* it?

10. Repeat it. Iterate on your intention statement time and again.

Let's analyze each step.

1. Position it from the positive

Ever notice when somebody says something like, "Whatever you do, don't think of…" that you immediately think of it? The same thing applies here.

When you frame a new intention, frame it from the positive ("I want to…") rather than the negative ("I don't want to…") to help your brain search for the right criteria.

I've said this before and I'll say it again: our brains will find whatever we're looking for, so make sure you feed it the right information from the right perspective.

Examples of **negative** positioning:

- "I don't want to get nervous before going on stage." If you think about getting nervous, you'll become nervous

- "I'm trying not to swear." By focusing on what not to say, those thoughts are already at the forefront of your mind.

2. Stay in the *now*.

The word choice you use reflects one of three things: the past, the present, the future. A statement like, "I will be calm when I go on stage" creates a reality of what we want in future rather than the reality of who we are right now. Here are examples of powerful "in the now" statements (along with their less-powerful brethren):

Negative (Critical, Judgmental)	Not Present	Powerful
I should be…	I should…	I choose…
I have to be…	I have to…	I am…
Why can't I…	I choose to…	How can I…
I need to be…	I need to…	I am being…

Random Exercise
The Rubber Band Bracelet: Override Your Self-Limiting Beliefs

To neutralize the <u>self-limiting beliefs</u> that limit your potential, try the follow exercises:

For the next 24 hours, pay attention to your thoughts—not the ones telling you, "Damn I look good!" but the negative ones. I know, I know. I've said before *not* to focus on the negatives, but forget I said that for a second for the following reason:

You will get whatever you focus on.

In other words, by paying attention to the negative words that pass through your mind you become more aware they exist, and awareness is half the battle.

Once you're aware of the negative words themselves, do the following:

1) Jot down the word.

2) Notice the context that triggered the negative thought to arise. Write that down, too.

3) Keep a tally of both one and two.

As mentioned previously, what gets measured gets improved (with a little bit of effort), so by tracking what words appear, their periodicity, and the situational context associated with them, you now have ALL the information you need to 1) identify the problem and 2) solve the problem.

Here's how you do it.

Get a rubber band that fits around your wrist. Wear it everywhere. It doesn't matter how stupid you look. It benefits you so that's all that matters. Every time you notice another negative troll enter your mind, give yourself a good "snap!" on the wrist with your less-than-stylish rubber band. Over time, your brain will begin to predict the consequence of thinking negatively.

Now, to adapt any habit requires three things, and thinking is no different. First, a habit needs a cue—the impetus for subsequent behavior. The cue incites a routine (i.e. the negative thinking process) that ultimately leads to a reward. In this case, for instance, the reward for telling yourself you "can't speak in front of groups" is the relief of not having to do so. Although it's a subconscious win (since you are choosing not to publicly speak), the conscious ramification is a fear of public speaking that only snowballs into greater fear the more you tell yourself how scared you are.

What you want to do is replace the routine with another routine. Since you can't eliminate thinking (even if you've met people who seems like they have), you must replace the negative with the positive. That's how habits work.

If you don't replace the routine with another routine, then you're just acting on willpower. Willpower is a muscle and like every other muscle, it gets tired the more you use it.

So, every time that little devil of "I can't..." rears its ugly face, give yourself a big rubber brand bracelet "snap!" and turn that negative into a positive. Just say the exact opposite of the negative. If you just told yourself, for example, "I'm not good at..." let the self-masochist out of its cage for a brief second to remind your brain to stop saying such things, and then tell yourself, "I am good at…". What this does is build your self-identify so that you see yourself as the type of person who *can* achieve.

Do it for thirty days. You won't believe the progress you make in navigating uncertainty and building mental toughness.

3. Elevate your intention to its optimal level.

In her book Managing Thought, author Mary Lore gives a powerful example of stating an intention at its highest level by citing Dave Hopla, professional basketball shooting coach. Dave's guidance for his players in creating the intention to win is this: "The difference between being a good shooter and a great shooter is not to intend on *making* each shot but to intend on *swooshing* each shot."

Do you see the difference? By elevating your intention to its optimal level of success you create a mental rehearsal of winning.

4. Focus on *being* rather than *doing*.

The verb *To Do* connotes a degree of judgment along with it; an implicit criticism unbeknownst to its user. For example, the statement, "I'm *doing* everything I can to make it there in time" suggests a gap between where you are (currently) and where you want to be (destination), thereby yielding judgment in the discrepancy between the two and causing unwanted pressure.

However, if you replace this statement with, "I *am* making it there in time," you eliminate judgment, you eliminate pressure because you're just focused on the present.

Now, hear me out—I'm not saying ignore your deadlines. Of course there are places we need to be and Murphy sometimes likes to challenge our will in getting to those places. What I am saying, though, is that you can use this as a powerful mental exercise to reduce stress and focus only on what you can affect. You can't control traffic, you can't control others' behaviors. What you can control is how you perceive them, and this is an integral step to doing so.

5. Affirm your intention.

After you identify what your intention is, you want to affirm it by saying it to yourself. Use powerful words and phrases (see above) that connote individual choice rather than negative ones that suggest an external influence.

6. Experience your intention.

People see mentally what they experience most, so the degree to which you can incorporate the senses of feeling, smell, touch, sight, hearing, the better. Now, remember that this doesn't necessarily have to be in real time. In other words, since our brains don't know the difference between perception and reality, we can create those powerful "experiences" that haven't happened yet, but in which we intend to "win." It's not easy and it takes extreme focus, but it's exactly the sort of powerful driver that induces the emotion you want (since emotion drives behavior).

7. Write it.

An unwritten goal is just a dream. Writing out your intention serves as not just another experiential component, but also a way to hold yourself accountable as well as serve as a reminder.

If you really want to boost the likelihood of a powerfully written intention, share it with an accountability partner, friend, or colleague. I don't know about you but when I exercise with other people I always push myself harder, and I do so because two things are involved that don't exist when I workout in alone: judgment and responsibility.

8. Read it.

After you've written out you intention, read it aloud. Notice what you feel. Is it motivating? Engaging? Empowering? If not, have another go at it.

9. Remember it.

What did you notice when you read your intention aloud? What feelings passed through your body? What senses peaked? What words would you use to describe how your intention felt as you heard it? Use those words to create new anchors.

10. Repeat it.

Iterate on your intention statement time and time again.

Of course if those negative thoughts didn't exist in the first place then we wouldn't have to replace them, right? So, maybe it's not so much that we need to replace negative thoughts with positive ones since doing so is akin placing a band-aid on a cut. No, we don't want a band-aid, we want a cure. Here's what I mean.

To replace a negative thought with a positive means that we have already attributed some definition of success to [something]. If that "something" was an expectation for a job promotion but we didn't get it, then unhappiness seeps in and begins to inundate our once-happy thoughts. In other words, our expectation for happiness has been replaced with reality, and that reality sucks (i.e. unhappy).

Why is this important? Because we tend to associate happiness with being successful; that if we work harder, put in longer hours and spend more time making money that we'll ultimately be successful and with that success, comes new found happiness.

We place success at the center of the universe with degrees of happiness circling all around it; as if success is something that exists by itself and once we attain it, *then* we'll be happy and no negative thoughts will ever permeate our minds again.

We all know this not to be true, yet people ascribe to it all the time.

Why? Glad you asked.

How Happiness Helps

Nobody likes being a grumpy pants. But what may not be so obvious are the neurological implications of positivity upon the brain and subsequent behavior. Just as negative emotions constrain our thinking, positive ones enable it.

Research by Barbara Fredrickson reveals that positive emotions "open" the mind to greater creativity and "…discovery of novel and creative actions, ideas and social bonds, which in turn build that individual's personal resources; ranging from physical and intellectual resources, to social and psychological resources. Importantly, these resources function as reserves that can be drawn on later to improve the odds of successful coping and survival."[8]

A second key proposition concerns the consequences of these broadened mindsets: by broadening an individual's momentary thought-action repertoire, whether through play, exploration or similar activities, positive emotions promote discovery of novel and creative actions, ideas and social bonds, which in turn build that individual's personal resources ranging from physical and intellectual to social and psychological resources. Importantly, these resources function as reserves that can be drawn upon later to improve the odds of successful coping and survival.

Here are three more ways positive emotions enable us:

1. **They broaden our thought–action reserve.** In English, this means that people with positive emotions show patterns of thought that "are notably unusual, flexible, creative, integrative, open to information and efficient."[8]

2. **Positive emotions "undo" the negative leftovers.** Think of emotions in terms of weight, with positive ones weighing more than negative ones. Our brains seek pleasure and avoid pain, so to the extent that we can find pleasure, we will. Unfortunately, what this "pleasure" sometimes looks like is procrastination, doubt, victimization—clearly all negative emotions but pleasant to think about in the moment because they help us avoid having that difficult conversation, or facing our fears. The key is to switch how you think about the problem so you associate greater pleasure with it. This is the values that coaches bring: a shift in perspective—one that may not have been considered otherwise—that leads us to think differently (positively about "X").

3. **They fuel mental resiliency.** Note here that it's not physical resiliency but rather mental resiliency. Having positive emotions at your disposal serve as the mental fuel for a "can do" attitude, as we begin to draw upon positively emotive

experiences at opportune moments in order to cope with negative ones.

CHAPTER 7
UNDERSTANDING
THOUGHT
ARCHITECTURE

In Charles Duhigg's book The Power of Habit: Why We Do What We Do, and How to Change, he (ironically) cites how he developed a bad habit of his own: getting up from his desk at work to visit the snack bar and get a chocolate chip cookie.

What he didn't realize at the time was the domino effect this habit was creating, which looked a lot like an additional eight-pounds of weight and unsolicited comments from his spouse.

What did he do? He did what anybody else would do: he tried to "will" that bad habit away. He thought that by setting himself reminders in the form of post-it notes that read "no more cookies" he'd be able to stave off this newfound negative behavior. But it didn't work. It never does.

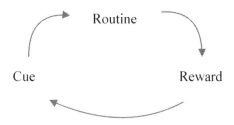

As mentioned previously, willpower is a muscle and muscles get tired. If you want to change a habit, you need to change how you think about "it" (whatever "it" is). In this case, the "it" was the cookie.

What does work, however, is understanding the thought architecture behind how habits work and developing a mental game plan for a new one. Here's how.

The Thought Architecture of Habits

In the 1990s, researchers at MIT discovered a neurological loop at the core of every habit. This loop consisted of three parts: a cue, a routine and a reward:

The **cue** is the stimulus. It tells your brain to forget everything else and automate behavior. The **routine** is the behavior itself (i.e. physical, mental, emotional). The **reward** is what the brain believes it will receive in exchange for that behavior. The more

often this cue – routine – reward cycle is repeated—
and the more pleasant the reward—the easier the
habit becomes ingrained into your daily behavior
and, therefore, subconscious.

Consider, for a moment, the internet and its vast
extent of knowledge. If you're an infopreneur (that's
somebody who constantly seeks more and more
information) and your habit is surfing the web "just
to see," then the cue that tells you to surf may be
boredom; your routine might be to go online and
search random "stuff," and the reward is the
exhilaration of learning something new (or *avoiding*
whatever you really had to do at the moment).

While learning is not exactly a bad habit, it's what
that "learning" is substituted for that is the root of
the problem. After all, how much from the internet
do you *actually* retain at the end of the day? I didn't
think so.

In this case, the quench for knowledge is a substitute
for whatever the unwanted activity is be it work, a
sales call, a difficult conversation. These are the cues
that cause us to immediately look elsewhere (i.e. the
internet) to avoid the mental and/or emotional pain
of dealing with reality.

Here's the problem. Our brains don't distinguish
between good and bad habits, which is why breaking
bad habits is so difficult. We're in a constant tug-of-

war match between the part of the brain that just wants to "feel good" and the other, more logical side that says, "No, this doesn't make sense."

The good news is, by understanding thought architecture, you can reengineer how your habits work.

Here's a four step method to break a bad habit:

1.   Identify the routine
2.   Experiment with rewards
3.   Isolate the cue
4.   Have a plan

Let's start this off by reframing the situation into something more fun. Imagine you're a (mad) scientist running experiments and you want to try a new habit on yourself (doesn't that sound fun?). With that, you'll want to divide it into four phases.

Phase 1: Identify the Routine

You should already know what your routine is (that's the behavior you want to change). If, for instance, you want to eliminate snacking on your child's leftovers then you would put that in the routine stage of the habit loop.

Next, you want to identify what your cue and reward are for this routine.

Phase 2: Experiment with Rewards

Rewards are powerful because they satisfy our cravings. Our brains want two things and two things only: to find pleasure and to avoid pain. That's it. The trick is to reframe those behaviors that once constituted "pain" (mental, emotional, spiritual) into pleasure-seeking behaviors.

Try this. When you feel the urge to perform your bad habit, change your routine so it delivers a different reward. For example, if your bad habit is eating sugar, try eating an apple instead.

The next time the cue to reach for sugary, crap food arises, do the same.

If that apple isn't doing the trick, try an orange (but not orange juice—there's enough sugar in orange juice to kill an elephant).

Important: The goal here is to test different hypotheses to determine what the **cue** is that's driving your routine. It's not find substitute rewards.

Be sure to look for patterns in behavior. In fact, write on a piece of paper or your phone the first three things that come to mind when thinking of your reward. These can be emotions or thoughts on how you're feeling or just the first three words that enter your mind.

Then set an alarm on your phone for fifteen minutes. This is to identify the reward you're craving. When it goes off, ask yourself, "Do I still feel the urge to do my bad habit?"

To return to the above example, if you're still craving sugar after eating an apple then your craving isn't motivated by hunger (otherwise, your craving would've been satisfied). Rather, it's motivated by a different reward.

If, however, you called a friend and at the end of your 15 minutes and you no longer craved sugar, then it was diverting attention away from your activity of the moment that was your reward.

The next step is to ask yourself what about that cue causes you to behave the way you do. Is it a mundane job? Personality conflicts? Lack of fulfillment? Again, write down three things that come to mind.

The reason why it's important to write down three things is because:

1. **It builds awareness.** By capturing what we're thinking and feeling in the moment we build awareness—and resilience—toward the cue itself.

2. **It helps track progress.** If you don't capture what you were thinking or feeling at a given moment, chances are you'll never remember. This is important to reflect upon for future situations where the environment may incite similar thoughts or feelings. By having the context to know how you've reacted in the past, you can better anticipate how you want to react in the future. You can also better anticipate environmental changes because you're building up your own situational awarenes.

3. **It isolates the reward**. By experimenting with different rewards, you can isolate the reward (i.e. pleasure) you're actually craving rather than the reward you think you're craving. This is essential to reengineering your habit.

Phase 3: Isolate the Cue

In BUD/S, the obstacle course served as a natural laxative. Just the thought of waiting your turn to run it compelled not just me, but every student to, well, feel like they had to run...right to the bathroom.

What the o-course represents here are cues that incite immediate responses. Have you ever been somewhere that just "made" you feel sad? How about a date—a particular time of day—that spurred the same thought? Or what about the social handgrenades that exist—the kind of people you avoid like the plague because just the mere thought of them instigates feelings of annoyance? These are all cues that may not necessarily be physically experienced, but just the mere thought of them is strong enough to incite an emotional response.

This is why it's difficult to kick a bad habit. There are myriad cues working *against* us at any given time which is why, in order to break that bad habit, you must consider multiple possibilities for what that cue might be.

When you feel your bad habit about to ensue, consider the following questions to try to isolate the cue:

1. Location. Where are you? What are you doing?

2. Time. What time of day is it?

3. Feelings. What is your emotional state right now? How do you feel? What words would you use to describe it?

4. People. What are the social influences of your situation? Who else is around?

5. Previous. What were you doing immediately before your urge came on?

Do this for a week and look for repeat responses, recurring patterns. For example, if you notice by the fifth day you've written down "lack of fulfillment" for emotional state all seven times, then a lack of fulfillment is probably your cue.

Phase 4: Have a Contingency Plan

Hopefully by now you've isolated the cue that ignites your unwanted behavior. The next step is to visualize what you will do the next time that cue appears, and the most effective way to do this is through **if-then planning**. It's very simple, and very powerful—two of my favorite characteristics. If-then planning looks like this:

If **X** happens, then I will do **Y**.

If-then planning is a powerful way to establish a backup plan if/when your initial plan fails because it's encoded in a language that our brains already understand.

In fact, if-then planners are approximately 300 percent MORE likely to reach their goals than their no-plan counterparts.

The reason is because our brains look for two things: pleasure and avoidance of pain, and it looks simultaneously.

So, **if** pleasure cannot be sought **then** it looks for the next source of pleasure while avoiding every possible source of pain out there.

In other words, if-then planning is a natural process our brains cycle through because contingency planning is already built into our neurological wiring.

Humans are very good at encoding information in an "if x, then y" format and using those connections (often unconsciously) to guide their behavior. When people decide exactly when, where, and how they will fulfill their goals, they create a link in their brains between a certain situation or cue ("If or when x happens") and the behavior that should follow ("then I will do y").

In this way, they establish powerful triggers for action; they essentially create a habit almost instantly.

Consider the following example…

A recent review of results from 94 studies that used the if-then technique found significantly higher success rates for almost every goal you can think of, including monthly breast self-examination, test preparation, using public transportation instead of driving, buying organic foods, being more helpful to others, avoiding alcohol, not smoking, losing weight, recycling, negotiating fairly, avoiding stereotypic or prejudicial thoughts, and better time management.

In fact, one study examined people whose goal was to exercise regularly. Half the participants were asked to plan where and when they would exercise each week (i.e., "**If** it is Monday, Wednesday, or Friday, **then** I will hit the gym for an hour before work.") while the other group did not.

The results were dramatic. Months later, 91percent of if-then planners were still exercising regularly, compared to only 39percent of non-planners.

Spike the mic, walk away.

PLANNING FOR THE UNKNOWN

If-then planning is especially useful for dealing with the inevitable hiccups posed by Murphy that lead to unforeseen complications, catastrophes and confusion.

Studies show that people who choose in advance how they will manage themselves when facing these ugly bumps in the road are much more resilient and focused than those who don't anticipate their (re)actions at all.

Here's how to begin. Start by **identifying risks**. Whenever we planned a mission in the SEALs we did so based off the intel we had, and we always had to consider three courses of action they enemy *could* take:

- their most capable course of action

- their least capable course of action

- what we believed would ensue

Start with the most capable course(s) of action first because you will quickly see the extent of your available resources, such as time, money, resources, etc...If, for instance, your goal is to generate greater decision making within your team, what would be the most capable course(s) of action for success? That is, what would set up the team to succeed? Alternatively, what wouldn't? What would the strongest likelihood (by you, another team member, the market, or a competitor) be that would prevent the team from achieving this goal? Write these down so you see them.

Next, you'll want to breakdown each component into actionable next steps *if* that situation arises.

So, to continue with the mission planning scenario above, *if* the enemy isn't armed but is still non-compliant, *then* we will do [insert action here]. By identifying the action to take should one of those risks turn into a reality, you know automatically what your response will be which 1) decreases your response time and therefore 2) increases the likelihood of you achieving your goal.

Here's a flow chart to better visualize what this process looks like:

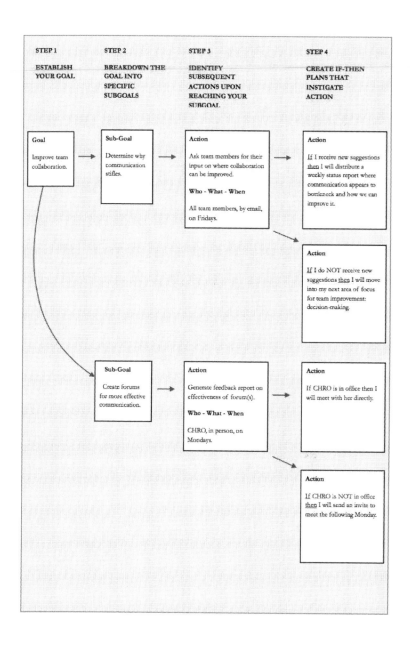

STEP 1

ESTABLISH
YOUR GOAL

STEP 2

BREAKDOWN THE
GOAL INTO
SPECIFIC
SUBGOALS

STEP 3

IDENTIFY
SUBSEQUENT
ACTIONS UPON
REACHING YOUR
SUBGOAL

STEP 4

CREATE IF-THEN
PLANS THAT
INSTIGATE
ACTION

Goal

Improve team collaboration.

Sub-Goal

Determine why communication stifles.

Action

Ask team members for their input on where collaboration can be improved.

Who - What - When

All team members, by email, on Fridays.

Action

If I receive new suggestions then I will distribute a weekly status report where communication appears to bottleneck and how we can improve it.

Action

If I do NOT receive new suggestions then I will move into my next area of focus for team improvement: decision-making.

Sub-Goal

Create forums for more effective communication.

Action

Generate feedback report on effectiveness of forum(s).

Who - What - When

CHRO, in person, on Mondays.

Action

If CHRO is in office then I will meet with her directly.

Action

If CHRO is NOT in office then I will send an invite to meet the following Monday.

CHAPTER 8

23 EXERCISES FOR NAVIGATING THE CHAOS

OF THE MOMENT

1. Focus on the present.

One of the biggest derailers toward losing the mental edge is letting your focus slip. Big keys to success for any golfer is her ability to keep her thoughts present-centered throughout a round. Allowing your thoughts to drift to the past or get ahead of you can be a significant distraction.

Professional golfer Michelle Wie mentioned how she transformed her mental strategy for performing under pressure:

When you focus on the present, you prepare yourself for thoughtful and intentional execution.

2. Create an anchor.

Think for a minute about your favorite song. What is it? How does it make you feel? Everyone has a favorite tune that jazzes them up during a workout, quells their nerves after a long day, or otherwise alters their emotional state. This is called anchoring.

An anchor is a thought, a smell, a physical touch, an area of focus on which we spend our time that immediately takes your mind elsewhere—good or bad—and instigates a new feeling. You can create anchors in two ways:

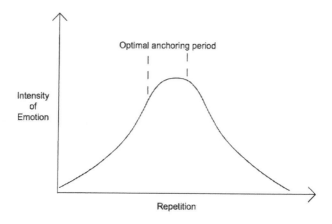

1) Heightened emotion

2) Repetition

Remember Pavlov's dog and how that poor little pooch began to salivate at the mouth at the mere sound of hearing the bell ring? That's anchoring— and yes, you can do it for yourself. Here's how.

To build an anchor, close your eyes and think of the happiest time in your life. I mean REALLY consider EVERYTHING about it—not just the obvious things like the smells, the sentiment, how you felt, but how your ears drew back because your smile was so large; how your heartbeat was slightly higher than normal due to all the excitement (and what *was that excitement?*). You get the idea. REALLY focus here on as much detail as possible so you can remember as much as possible and replicate that happy moment again.

Now, once you have this "happy place" identified and the intensity of the memory is peaked, take your right index finger and rub it back and forth on top of your right middle finger. This is your physical anchor. Repeat this several times.

Congratulations, you now have an anchor. The more you repeat this exercise, the more ingrained into your subconscious it becomes. To activate that anchor, simply repeat the physical sequence you used when you imagined the event—in this case, it's the rubbing of your fingers.

Anchors are powerful because they can create lasting habits. This is why you see boxers, basketball players, and other professionals wearing headphones on the way to the locker room on game day. They're not "jamming" to look cool (okay, maybe some are), they're listening to the same playlist, the same songs, in the same order to get into the "zone"—their happy place—and they do so consistently, which brings me to the next exercise…

3. Perform a Cognitive (Re-)Appraisal

A cognitive appraisal is the mental process that enables us to define what is happening *to* us or *around* us as drawn from our family upbringing, role models, values, traits, fears and hopes. For example, a mediocre performance review at work upsets you on Monday, but by Wednesday you think it's actually pretty good. You're angry about a parking ticket in the afternoon but by the next day you realize it's no big deal. You wake up in the middle of the night in a panic about something, but by morning it doesn't feel so bad. What changed? You still have to pay the ticket, and the performance appraisal still stands. What's changed is how you now appraise the event: "This isn't fair" has become "Well, I deserved the ticket," or "I am going to get fired has transformed" to "The review wasn't that bad; I'm just disappointed, but I can improve." The fact that you can change your appraisals of a situation allows you to regulate the pressure you experience. Moreover, two people can appraise the same situation differently. You might see giving a presentation as a threat or crisis whereas a teammate sees it as an opportunity.

An appraisal can also be skewed by your state of mind in the moment. Being angry or sad will create a different interpretation of the situation than feeling hopeful or energetic. The good news is, you can choose your emotional state. Happy, sad, depressed or stressed, *you choose* how you "show up." Make that choice count.

4. The Pressure Of Acceptance.

We don't worry about letting others down per se—we worry about others accepting or rejecting us. Therefore the stronger an individual's need is for acceptance and approval, the more pressure he or she is likely to experience in these situations. This effect is so powerful that it can impact high-pressure performers at the most competitive levels, including, as we've seen, the top golfers in the world. Students who have a high need for parental approval also report feeling more pressure to perform academically than those who rate high on self-acceptance.

5. Word Choice—Choose Carefully.

Pay attention to the word choices you make. Simple words like "need" or "must" increase the feeling of pressure and are more reactive in nature, whereas proactive word choices tell your mind there's a choice, thereby eliminating the sense of "external" pressure. Common differences include:

Reactive
- "I need to..."
- "I have to…"
- "I must…"
- "I can't…"

Proactive

- "I choose to..."
- "I will…"
- "I want to…"

6. Ranking vs. Excellence Mindsets

➤ Ranking Mindset
- Characterized by a win-at-all-costs approach driven by insecurity and the need to prove oneself.
- It is about proving they are "better" than another person.

➤ Excellence Mindset
- Focused on maximizing your potential
- Views competition as an opportunity to improve— not as a way to prove *they* are better than someone else, but as a way of challenging *themselves.*

Consequences Of A Ranking-Mindset

It causes greater physical arousal in the body because the ranking mind keeps you on edge—you always have to be ready for the "fight," always ready to beat your competitor. It also:

- impairs decision-making

- leads to regret (as a matter of poor decision-making)

Don't get me wrong, I'm all for competition. But when you define your self-worth by the result rather than the effort applied, *that's* when disappointment sets in.

7. Appraise The Situation

Whenever you feel uncertainty on the rise, ask yourself the following questions:

1. Does the situation really call for the reaction I am having?
2. Am I wearing myself out by overreacting when I don't need to?
3. Can my performance in this situation actually threaten my success?

Your answers will help you gauge whether you are *really* in a situation where there is stress and pressure (think of being in a gunfight) or where you are merely feeling stressed. Here's an example:

"When the pressure spikes like this, I start feeling like I'm not getting enough done and I feel overwhelmed. If I am not managing the pressure, then I start responding to e-mails right away, being more reactive, and I can have an impact on people I don't want to have. It affects my leadership and the performance of my team. And it's not just in business— it's in my personal life, too. If a friend texts me and I don't get back to them in ten minutes, I get another text saying 'Is everything okay?' At this point I feel like I am going to implode and now I start impacting my key personal relationships, too."

It is the everyday pressure of "having" to succeed that causes a trader to ignore and violate trading regulations or "causes" the student to cheat. It isn't just the pressure of the presentation before the CEO or the senior team; it is the constant pressure to execute, to achieve the year's sales or revenue goals and to get the annual bonus that causes managers to contemplate doing something unethical. Just look at Wells Fargo[3].

If you missed one of the larger news headlines of 2016, the largest U.S. bank by stock value, Wells Fargo, was hit with fines amounting to just under $200 million for its rogue sales behavior. Five thousand three hundred employees allegedly opened customer accounts—on the sly—to boost sales figures, leading to excessive—and unknown— account holder fees.

[3] Adopted from my Forbes column

Let me repeat that: 5,300 employees.

Now, of course sales teams have to be aggressive because they're commission-based which means they eat what they kill.
However, there's a line between ethical and unethical that Wells Fargo employees clearly crossed, and they crossed it not because the values didn't exist within the company—Wells Fargo's vision and values clearly express trust as an important bedrock—but because of how they appraised the situation. Namely, there was no accountability in enforcing those values, and without *some* structure, there's chaos.

Don't get me wrong, there shouldn't be a need to enforce "right" because people should already know what "right" looks like. Honesty, trust and integrity are just a few of the values that should be *expected* rather than aspired for.

However, it's clear that not one of these 5,300 employees was held accountable during their misbehavior (and don't tell me nobody else knew— 5,300 isn't exactly a small number). It's also clear that Wells Fargo's leaders and managers set themselves up for failure by not instituting a culture of curiosity. Here's what I mean.

My business partner has been in sales for over 15 years. One problem he's seen across sales organizations is a lack of clarity from leadership on a vision for change and the associated objectives needed to support that change. A recent study[4] on change management and sales training intervention confirms this, stating that only 51percent of sales leaders communicate a vision for change. This leaves a significant portion of sales teams blinded by chaos with no clear pathway out, simply because they lack the guidance—the vision—from senior leaders.

When it comes to improving sales performance management, organizations obsessed with the curiosity of constant improvement never settle for *what is* because they're constantly on the lookout for *what might be better.*

However, that's not all. When it comes to teams, the sales "teams" at Wells Fargo are anything but team-centric. Consider the following in the context of "appraising the situation" and think for a moment about how you would respond:

No shared mission. A team is not a team without a shared definition of success. Without all efforts aligned toward the same purpose, you have a group of individuals working closely beside each other but

[4] https://assets.adobe.com/link/0e511008-b9c6-4057-7a2a-12d707e62b67

not together. The 5,300 Wells Fargo employees were incentivized to make as much money as possible *as individuals*, but not as a team. A shared mission is just that—shared. It's an incentive that defines the *team's* success and appraises the situation in a *we* rather than *me* context. Without each team member bound to a shared purpose, there's no need *to* be accountable because they can keep being individuals without repercussions.

Here's what typically happens. A sales "team" incentivizes each member to close as many deals as possible and the winner receives a reward. That's not exactly teaming. Where's the shared purpose? You can't possibly create a shared purpose if each member is incentivized to chase after rewards that acknowledge only his or her efforts. In the military, when our mission changed from counterterrorism to counterinsurgency, for example, we found ourselves with a new definition of success. No longer was the number of raids we conducted or enemy killed a criterion for success. Instead, the new metric was how many civilians we saved. What this did was it changed behavior *at scale*. You can't motivate the masses, there are just too many people and too many interests. What you can do, however, is set the right environment for such motivations to occur. This way, people's behaviors must change because they need to align their daily actions with the new definition of success.

No accountability. People often view being held accountable as blame or accusation, and that's because they don't trust the other person to have positive intentions. Accountability shows up in one of three ways:

1. Top-down. This is when the boss is accountable for his or her team (typically a sign of an ordinary, but not an extra-ordinary, team).

2. Bottom-up. Accountability from the bottom-up means team members hold each other accountable and question the status quo. High performing teams are accountable from the bottom up.

3. Non-existent. Just like avoiding to make a decision is still a decision, somebody is still accountable for a lack of accountability. There's no such thing as zero accountability. There is, however, such a thing as unenforced accountability, which is exactly what happened among Wells Fargo management.

No trust. Accountability suffers when people don't trust others' intentions. In cultures of low trust there are silos, turf wars and behind-the-back snickering because people don't trust each other to say or do the right thing, so it forces people to protect their own self-interests. If this is your environment, what impacts do you think this situational appraisal will have upon you and your performance? In the case of Wells Fargo, it drove 5,300 employees to choose *wrong* over *right*.. Environment is everything.

The thing is, a lack of trust has far wider organizational impacts. Without trust you can't get work accomplished as quickly because you don't trust the other person to execute successfully. There are also duplicative efforts associated with low trust which lead to higher costs.

Here's a good rule of thumb to test your team's level of performance from low to high performing. If it takes longer than a day for your team to resolve problems, then your team isn't high performing. Generally speaking, the longer it takes to resolve an issue from the time that issue arises, the less effective the team is because in that time gap is where snickering, politicking and wasted costs ensue. Give it a try.

Breeding trust begins first by extending trust. After all, why should anybody trust you if you're unwilling to trust them?

8. Beat Pressure With Self-Awareness

People who handle pressure well are also sensitive to their physiological arousal "shifts," which allows them to regulate their arousal by, for instance, breathing slower, which enables them to process information more effectively and prevent themselves from becoming mentally rigid, thus preventing counterproductive, impulsive, defensive comments, all products of unmanaged physical arousal. Regulating arousal is crucial if you are going to manage emotions such as anxiety and fear that usually accompany pressure and make you do worse.

By bringing insight into how high-pressure situations make you feel, and reflect on the thoughts that are generating those feelings, you will have a better chance of not allowing your emotions to sabotage your decision-making, which subsequently impacts your performance.

9. Reframe Pressure As Opportunity

The biggest obstacle that individuals face in using pressure solutions is their inability to free themselves from past responses. When these ineffective past pressure responses become habitual, they resurface without the individual's awareness in a high-pressure situation. To prevent yourself from being held hostage by past responses, use the feelings of pressure that you experience as a cue that it is time to employ one or more of the pressure solutions found in this chapter. Remember that the experience is enjoyable and exciting rather than uncomfortable and unsettling. Positive arousal translates into enthusiasm, which is a powerful emotion in overcoming anxiety and fear. Think of the high-pressure situations you've been in and the times you've performed well. You were probably enjoying the moment despite the pressure.

10. Build Your "Challenge Thinking"

The difference between "go-getters" and everyone else is this: go-getters see opportunity where others see obstruction; they view obstacles as a challenge to overcome rather than a minefield to avoid. To build you "challenge thinking," try the following exercise:

Think of your tasks and responsibilities as daily challenges to strut your stuff. If you are a project manager, tell your team, "I challenge you to make this your best work ever." A sales manager might tell his sales force, "Here's the challenge— let's see if we are up to it." Or "Hey, it's great that we get opportunities like this to show how good we are!"

Reframe an obstacle into a challenge and you'll be surprised how much opportunity you find. Speaking of which...

11. Expect Opportunity

In one study, a group of auto mechanics were told they had one chance to demonstrate their ability to assemble an engine that they had been practicing on for the previous two weeks. To increase the pressure on them, they were told that if they assembled it correctly within the time allotted, they would be in line for a supervisory position they all desired.

A second group was given the same task and the same promise of promotion, but they were also told that if they made mistakes that they would be given additional opportunities to show their competence. The results? The group with only one chance felt more pressure, made more mistakes, and took longer to assemble the engine. The fact is, it is actually realistic to think that additional opportunities will come your way—because they do. Now, this is not to say that you shouldn't seize the moment when moments of opportunity arise. Yes, absolutely do that! However, I'm also of the opinion that whatever happens as a result of seizing said opportunity is a win because one of two things will happen:

1) You "achieve" (whatever the opportunity was)

2) You learn (if you don't "achieve" what you wanted, you certainly learned something from it which can be applied to the next opportunity. That's a win.)

12. Nerves Of Steel: Minimize The Importance Of The Moment

Pressure distorts our perceptions often to an irrational view of the moment, and this distorted thinking downgrades our cognitive success tools, such as judgment and decision-making, and motivates impulsive behavior.

Exercise: be mindful of what is most important in your life. Making a list will help you. Right before a pressure moment, reflect on your "most important" list— it will help you keep your current moment in proper pressure perspective. Of course we recognize that a pressure moment is defined as *important*, but it's also important not to exaggerate its significance.

13. Focus, Focus, Focus

Different situations will dictate the means by which you focus. Generally speaking, you can focus on the end state of success itself or the process that gets you there. In high pressure moments, you want to focus on the process rather than the outcome.

Focusing on the outcome steers your thinking into whether or not you will suffer negative consequences if you *don't* succeed; worrying over failure can distract and derail you. In contrast, focusing on the process creates a mind-set that helps you recognize the best way to accomplish your mission is to simply do your best at each step along the way. In this way, you stay anchored in the moment.

14. Find Control

For many of us— athletes and employees as well— a pressure moment can undermine our performance because we focus on factors we can't control. When you focus on "uncontrollables" you intensify the pressure because it boosts your anxiety to the point of disturbing your physiology, creating distracting thoughts that undermine your confidence. If you want a shot at being your best when it matters most, apply this pressure solution before and during a high-pressure situation:

FOCUS ON WHAT YOU CAN CONTROL AND DISREGARD THE REST.

When you do this, you will have reached a superpower. Seriously, it's completely liberating to not worry about things outside your control.

> *The only difference between people with low self-esteem and people with higher self-esteem is where they direct their focus.*

To execute this pressure solution effectively, you must know:

What you can control

What you cannot control

When your focus shifts to things you can't control, so you can snap it back.

Practice the following procedure to bring a focused mindset to bear during high-pressure moments:

Sitting in a comfortable chair, practice this three-minute procedure once a day for the next two weeks:

1) Identify an upcoming high-pressure scenario or one that you frequently encounter.
2) List the factors involved that you cannot control.
3) List the factors involved that you can control.
4) Visualize the high-pressure moment; think about the things you can control, and imagine those going well.
5) Now think about the things you can't control.
6) Visualize your performance going astray.
7) Bring your mind back into focus on what you can control, and visualize yourself getting back on track.

Points of performance: Tune in to the obvious such as your responses to the things you can control— your thoughts, physical arousal, and actions. These are the factors that determine how you perform.

15. Anchor Away!

Think of a high-pressure situation you've experienced recently. Next, visualize the task you had to perform. If it was a sales call, visualize yourself interacting with your client, speaking about your products; think about how and where you are sitting, and other details that give you a complete picture of the scene. Now come up with one word or image to broadly describe the best way to perform what you do. One reason many people do poorly in pressure moments is that they tend to overthink what they are doing. This self-consciousness distracts them from the task at hand, and performance suffers.

16. Disrupt feedback.

We talked earlier about the neuroscience of change and how the brain and body get caught in a fixed feedback loop where each is telling the other one what it wants but neither one is hearing it.

The only way to break out of that cycle and calm yourself down is to interrupt that feedback loop, and you can do so using the following process.

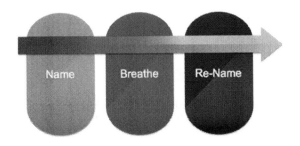

The arrow in the diagram above becomes less and less pronounced the more you travel along its path. The dark contrast, in this diagram, represents emotion.

Step 1: Name your emotions.

This is a trick I use in my coaching practice because it forces you to assign an identity to fear.

Let me ask you something.

Would fear of the unknown still exist if you knew what that unknown was? That is, would you still feel the emotional paralysis associated with uncertainty?

Maybe.

But I'm willing to bet you'd also feel more inclined to take a step toward the unknown because now you have a working definition. Now, every step you take just confirms or denies the name you assigned to that emotion.

By naming the fear (or rather the emotion behind that fear), you essentially "hack" the trepidation associated with the unknown and interrupt your brain's processing. It's as if the brain is intent on telling you one thing but you interrupt it by telling it, "No, what you're telling me isn't right. It's [this]!" and in return the brain says, "Huh? What did you say??"

Pretty cool, huh? Check out the chart on the next page to build your emotional-word-choice repertoire.

Intensity of Feeling Chart

	Happy	Sad	Angry	Confused	Afraid	Weak	Strong	Guilty
High	Elated	Depressed	Furious	Bewildered	Terrified	Helpless	Powerful	Sorrowful
	Excited	Disappointed	Enraged	Trapped	Horrified	Hopeless	Aggressive	Remorseful
	Overjoyed	Alone	Outraged	Troubled	Scared stiff	Beat	Gung Ho	Ashamed
	Thrilled	Hurt	Aggravated	Desperate	Petrified	Overwhelmed	Potent	Unworthy
	Exuberant	Left Out	Irate	Lost	Fearful	Impotent	Super	Worthless
	Ecstatic	Dejected	Seething		Panicky	Small	Forceful	
	Fired up	Hopeless				Exhausted	Proud	
	Delighted	Sorrowful				Drained	Determined	
Medium	Cheerful	Heartbroken	Upset	Disorganized	Scared	Dependant	Energetic	Sorry
	Up	Down	Mad	Foggy	Frightened	Incapable	Capable	Lowdown
	Good	Upset	Annoyed	Misplaced	Threatened	Lifeless	Confident	Sneaky
	Relieved	Distressed	Frustrated	Disoriented	Insecure	Tired	Persuasive	
	Satisfied	Regret	Agitated	Mixed up	Uneasy	Rundown	Sure	
	Contented		Hot		Shocked	Lazy		
			Disgusted			Insecure		
						Shy		
Mild	Glad	Unhappy	Perturbed	Unsure	Apprehensive	Unsatisfied	Secure	Embarrassed
	Content	Moody	Uptight	Puzzled	Nervous	Under par	Durable	
	Satisfied	Blue	Dismayed	Bothered	Worried	Shaky	Adequate	
	Pleasant	Sorry	Put out	Uncomfortable	Timid	Unsure	Able	
	Fine	Lost	Irritated	Undecided	Unsure	Soft	Capable	
	Mellow	Bad	Touchy	Baffled	Anxious	Lethargic		
	Pleased	Dissatisfied		Perplexed		Inadequate		

Step 2: Control your breathing.

When I was a junior in high school, my martial arts instructor taught me something so valuable that I still carry it with me to this day. He taught me how to manage my perspective and reframe negatives into positives by simply focusing on breathing. Discomfort, exhaustion, and pain of any sort are but temporary states along a much grander—and more permanent—continuum of *Being* (forgive me but, I'm about to get deep for a moment).

Your being—what makes you, *You,* such as your purpose, values, beliefs and vision—are ever-lasting. They may morph as time goes on and new experiences occur but they'll still be there; they'll still exist to define you.

Uneasiness does not define you. Nor do any of the other elements of discomfort mentioned above. Instead, they exist to *test* your being—they are random checks along the continuum of life that serve to test the strengths of your values, purpose, etc…When you answer the call and confront said uneasiness, you build a stronger you.

I remember my high school football team doing a track workout one day. The coach was trying to "motivate" us for making silly mistakes in the previous week's game, so we didn't know how long the workout was going to last or if there was anything else the coach had in store for us.

The workout was along a 400 meter track and it looked like this:

Jog the straightaway, sprint the curve. Repeat.

I have no idea how long we were out there but it felt like forever. As football players, our bodies weren't conditioned for endurance; we were prepared for short bursts of explosive power. So, an endurance workout to us was synonymous with "nightmare."

Our coach was tough. Telling us to "Run faster!" "Don't stop! If you stop we're gonna start over!"

Come to think of it, he would've made a great SEAL instructor.

This was a pivotal moment for me in terms of learning how to optimize my focus and manage the pressure of the unknown. Instead of slowing down because I was tired, I sped up. I found a mental space of comfort because I narrowed my focus from the expansive onslaught of the environment to what I could manage internally: my breathing.

I focused on the *process*.

If I had focused on the *endstate* of "When will this workout end?!" I would've been consumed by the negative.

By shifting my focus onto something that I could manage, I began to see the state of physical exhaustion as something that lasts only temporarily—and anything temporary just requires a stronger will or stronger skill to out-wait it. In this case, it was a test of will. I learned how to redefine what those temporary states meant in the moment so that I pursued them rather than avoided them; I saw them as challenges to conquer rather than burdens to avoid.

The more I focused on my breathing the more the physical pain vanished and the faster I became (or so it felt). I remember our coach, in addition to yelling the normal "Hurry up!" and all the expletives associated with it, he also began to yell, "We'll finish when Boss (yours truly) gets tired!" I don't say that out of arrogance but as a testament to the power of focusing on what you can control, and in this instance, what I *chose* to focus on was my breathing.

Anyways, I completely digressed from Step 2 (but I hope you got something out of that little story).

After interrupting the "brain" part of the feedback loop, you interrupt the "body" part by focusing on your breaths. In the SEAL Teams, I would do the following to quell my heartbeat and get myself under control:

Inhale to a count of four

Hold at the top to a count of four

Exhale to a count of four

Hold at the bottom to a count of four

Repeat

Why does this work? It works for two reasons:

1) It forces the brain to focus

2) It forces oxygen into your lungs and into your bloodstream which circulates back through the brain to tell it, "Hey, everything's okay."

Step 3: Re-label your emotions.

And you thought we were done talking about emotions, didn't you? Well, that's exactly what this step is about: eliminating negative emotions and replacing them with positive ones.

Go back to step one and review the labels you assigned your emotions (i.e. nervous, fearful, worried, etc...). Now, turn each negative into a positive. It may look like this:

From...	To...
• Nervous	• Excited
• Fearful	• Challenged
• Worried	• Aware

By re-naming your emotions, you are speaking right to the amygdala (the part of your brain that activates the fight - flight - freeze switch) and telling it to keep its hand *off* that switch; to instead, sit back and let the "storm" pass.

I'm not gonna lie, this takes practice. Try it for a month. I guarantee you'll see positive results.

17. Compartmentalize.

I know I've said before that you can't compartmentalize emotion, and that's true. Who you are at work is the same person who shows up at home. There is no such thing as work/life balance, only work/life integration.

However, what you can compartmentalize is your focus. Here's what I mean.

I'm going to use sports as an example here. Why? Because I'm a guy and that's what we do.

When you're playing on the field, the court, or the mat, where's your focus? Is it on the crowd? Is it on that kid in the third row who just picked his nose and wiped it on the bench? No. Your focus is on *the game*; it's on *winning* and the how you're going *to* win (i.e. the process).

The same is true no matter what endeavor you pursue. Even the seemingly benign projects you work on all day at the office, don't those require the same level of focus? Of course they do.

Instead, we allow distractions to override our focus. We set ourselves up for failure by choosing to work in a "fun" or "sporty" environment rather than in a productive one.

Who's fault is this? (Hint: it rhymes with "mine.")

It's been said before that what we focus on is what we get, so the degree that you can compartmentalize your focus on the task at hand is the extent to which you'll see results.

Here's the bad news. I can't teach this to you—the process of doing so, that is. This is only something that <u>you</u> can employ through self-awareness and self-discipline. Yes, it does take self-discipline—but so did playing on the court or whatever other sport you played.

18. Exercise.

If the benefits of exercise have been unclear in the past (they shouldn't; they're everywhere), here's yet another "win" for the physical fitness realm: activity is crucial to the way we think and feel.

Toxic levels of stress erode the connections between the billions of nerve cells in the brain and chronic depression is known to shrink certain areas of the brain. What does that mean? It means that we're getting dumber. Just kidding.

But the fact remains that stress can reduce certain parts of the brain, and it's also now known that exercise unleashes a cascade of neurochemicals and growth factors that can reverse this shrinking process, thus physically bolstering the brain's infrastructure. In fact, the brain responds much like muscles do: growing with activity, depleting with inactivity. The neurons in the brain connect to one another through "leaves" on treelike branches, and exercise causes those branches to grow and bloom with new buds, thus enhancing brain function at a fundamental level.

The body was designed to be pushed, and in pushing our bodies we push our brains too.

Exercise improves learning on three levels. **First**, it optimizes our alertness. We are more attentive when we have more energy, and exercise increases energy supplies. The shift of blood flow back to the brain (rather than the muscles that were being stressed) happens almost immediately after you finish exercising, which means this is the perfect time to focus on something that warrants sharp focus and complex thinking.

Second, exercise prepares and encourages nerve cells to bind to one another. The more connections we have the wider our net of knowledge is cast throughout the brain. This is the layman's terms equivalent of saying that nerve-cell binding is the cellular basis for registering new information.

Finally, exercise spurs the development of new nerve cells so our brains *can* learn more.

Nerd Alert #4

"A notable experiment in 2007 showed that cognitive flexibility improves after just one thirty-five-minute treadmill session at either 60 percent or 70 percent of maximum heart rate. The forty adults in the study (ages 50 to 64) were asked to rattle off alternative uses for common objects, like a newspaper— it's meant for reading, but it can be used to wrap fish, line a birdcage, pack dishes, and so forth. Half of them watched a movie and the other half exercised, and they were tested before the session, immediately after, and again twenty minutes later. The movie watchers showed no change, but the runners improved their processing speed and cognitive flexibility after just one workout. Cognitive flexibility is an important executive function that reflects our ability to shift thinking and to produce a steady flow of creative thoughts and answers as opposed to a regurgitation of the usual responses.

The trait correlates with high-performance levels in intellectually demanding jobs. So if you have an important afternoon brainstorming session scheduled, going for a short, intense run during lunchtime is a smart idea."

- From the book *Spark: The Revolutionary New Science Of Exercise And The Brain*

19. Phone a friend.

Not really. This is just a catchy sub-title. But of course, it does have meaning...

In advanced SERE (survival, escape, resistance, evasion) school, you learn how to survive and resist an enemy capture. For 36 hours you are placed in a two foot by two foot by seven foot box where you are told not to move; that if you fall asleep "you'll pay;" where the psychological games of being separated from your teammates is leveraged against you (and everyone else) to determine who is the weakest link.

The physical separation from each other goes against everything we (SEALs) know—that everything occurs *as a team*—and is used as a leverage point to induce stress.

Think about it. The human need for affiliation, for relationships is strong, and when you diminish or, even worse, destroy the accessibility to that need, it becomes a severe detriment to performance—individual and team.

Now, apply this concept to business, where cubicles and silos are the norm.

> "Boundaryless behavior is the soul of today's organization...People seem compelled to build layers and walls between themselves and others...These walls cramp people, inhibit creativity, waste time, vision, smother dreams, and above all slow things down."
>
> - Jack Welch, GE Chairman, 1981-2001

When we're isolated from each other, when our priorities are misaligned with what we value, when there is uncertainty as to what the next step should be, a message is sent in our brains to warn the amygdala of a threat in our environment; to essentially "brace for impact!" This message may come in different sizes, or levels of priority. For instance, if you're walking down the sidewalk and see somebody who "looks out of place," that message may be akin to a post-it note, telling your brain to simply "beware." If, however, you're walking down that same sidewalk and a mugger jumps out of nowhere demanding your money, that message from your amygdala just turned into a much larger notice. When this happens, we experience additional physiological sensations such as sweaty palms, tunnel vision, or auditory exclusion.

No matter what environmental stressor presents itself, the amygdala gets involved—sometimes in a major way, sometimes in a lesser way. The point is, every day our amygdala is responding to threats of some sort—large, small, innocuous, or severe—and every day our brains are hurriedly trying to put out fires; to assess real threats and perceived threats.

As it, turns out that, the location in our brains where we feel physical pain is the same as where we feel all types of pain. It's called the Anterior Cingulate Cortex, and it's located in the frontal lobe of the brain. The frontal lobe is often referred to as housing the "executive functions," such as judgment, planning, decision-making, problem solving, strategic visioning.

What does this mean? It means that when we experience fear—of any kind—our ability to think is severely inhibited.

How often does fear show up in your life? Where does it show up? If fear is something that plagues you, you're not operating at full potential.

So when we get scared, we don't think as well. When people in our businesses get scared, they don't think as well either, and business suffers.

Here's the neurochemical process breakdown. We experience a threat, something that frightens us, or stress in anyway and the amygdala starts to send signals like...

- Epinephrine to the adrenals

- Adrenals send signals to the hypothalamus

- The Hypothalamus sends signals to the pituitary gland to release the stress hormone cortisol, and when cortisol gets involved, you've reached a new neurobiological milestone.

Here's what happens next.

According to Dr. John Ratey, associate clinical professor of psychiatry at Harvard Medical School and author of the book Spark: The Revolutionary New Science Of Exercise And The Brain:

> "Cortisol wears a number of different hats during the stress response, one of which is that of traffic cop for metabolism. Cortisol takes over for epinephrine and signals the liver to make more glucose available in the bloodstream, while at the same time blocking insulin receptors at nonessential tissues and organs and shutting down certain intersections so the fuel flows only to areas important to fight-or-flight. The strategy is to make the body insulin-resistant so the brain has enough glucose. Cortisol also begins restocking the shelves, so to speak, replenishing energy stores depleted by the action of epinephrine. It converts protein into glycogen and begins the process of storing fat. If this process continues unabated, as in chronic stress, the action of cortisol amasses a surplus fuel

supply around the abdomen in the form of belly fat...It also helps explain why constantly high levels of cortisol— due to chronic stress— make it hard to learn new material, and why people who are depressed have trouble learning. It's not just lack of motivation, it's because the hippocampal neurons have bolstered their glutamate machinery and shut out less important stimuli. They're obsessed with the stress."

The takeaway here is this: the more stress in your life, the more potential for fatty tissue to build up and the more difficult it is to learn. If you're not learning, you're not adapting; if you're not adapting, you're stagnating; if you're stagnating, you're just biding time towards irrelevance.

The cost to us as individuals, as teammates, as employees, and as organizational leaders is significant. The brain operates on a budget, meaning, that it can only handle so much stress before the flight - flight - freeze response is activated and cortisol gets involved. Then, it's too late. The impact of stress takes its toll. Remember, the brain allocates resources based on physiological *need* rather than *want*, and it does so by itself, not by us telling it.

What does this look like in everyday life? In an organizational setting? Think of all the tiny stressors that exist in your daily life—even your routine—and you begin to see why managing the mental game is so important.

20. Use Feedback Analysis

Feedback analysis is a sexy term for reflecting upon—and analyzing—your own decisions. It works like this…

Consider the next decision you're about to make and the expectation of that decision. What do you expect to occur as a result? Write down your projection and then revisit it in six to nine months asking yourself these three questions:

1) Was it accurate?
2) What, if anything, changed?
3) How did *you* change?

This is a very powerful tool to measure just how much our decisions impact not only our lives, but also the lives of others. It's also a great way to identify your own decision-making process. Remember, what gets measured gets improved, and if we make nearly 35,000 decisions every day, it's worth it to spend a little time optimizing that process.

21. Visualize. Write.

Athletes do it. High performers do it. Anybody who wants to take his or her performance to the next level engages in mental imagery; visualization that tricks the mind into believing an event has already occurred.

The purpose of visualization is to leverage our senses to (re)create an experience or event in the mind that tricks the brain into thinking it (the experience or event) is actually happening. That way, when that experience or event actually occurs, actions and reactions become automatic.

In any high pressure or highly stressful situation where time is of the essence, the more you can react without thinking, the better. Of course, those reactions need to be effective. A reaction without an intention is a "swing and a miss."

Visualization can be used in two different ways:
1) To revisit a past event
2) To anticipate a future event

Let's first look at why it's important to revisit past events.

As you might guess, I enjoy writing. It's a way for me to process past events and sort through their meanings. I've found that it's not so much recollecting previous events that's the goal as it is assigning meaning to each one. This way, I not only build context from past experiences that can be applied toward future ones but also get to choose how intentional I want to be in interpreting those events—a valuable tool that I apply in my <u>coaching practice</u>.

Here are three more ways revisiting the past through mental imagery and writing will help you improve the mental game:

1. **You gain clarity.** I've found writing to help me be more succinct when <u>delivering speeches</u> because I've had to think through

how one idea relates to another. Writing helps iron out the messiness of ideas that we all have in our brains. If we don't disentangle them, we run the risk of missing valuable connections.

2. **You build context.** As I mentioned above, by writing out your interpretations you find new connections that might not have been so easily discernible otherwise. In the military we did this through After Action Reports (AARs). After every major training block and every mission, we assembled all participants into a room to review three things:

- What was intended to happen?
- What actually happened?
- What caused the difference?

When you do this in a team environment, two things occur. **First,** you build shared context throughout the team, enabling each member to "see" better and anticipate action the next time they're in a similar situation. In other words, each member gets to see the whole forest rather than the few trees they're accustomed to focusing on.

Second, you reinforce interdependencies of the team. When Jonny understands what was going through Mike's head when he was in front of a doorway (or a customer), Jonny has greater situational context to pull from next time. Jonny's reality may have been different from Mike's reality but now they know of each other's realities, which means they know how to complement each other toward a shared mission.

3. **You improve your emotional intelligence.** By reflecting on the emotions of a past situation, you heighten your awareness of the feelings involved such that you can more easily identify them next time. This is key to building your emotional intelligence. Emotional intelligence is one's ability to identify and interpret emotions within oneself and others, and is typically considered the number one business advantage any leader can possess (and is also one of the main reasons why leaders hire executive coaches).

Now, let's look at the value of visualizing future events.

Do you remember the first sport you learned to play? Let's just say it was basketball. If I had given you a basketball and said, "Okay, dribble" you would have had no idea what I was talking about nor any idea what dribbling even meant. That's because there was no context to pull from, no visual reference from which to base your performance.

But, if I demonstrate what dribbling is, offer some pointers on how to do it before you even try it, you now have two things:

1) a visual reference of what "right" looks like
2) information on which to base your behavior.

Remember that at this point you've never even heard of dribbling, but, with the new mental imagery of what dribbling looks like in your head, you now have a standard of judgment off of which to base your performance.

When you use visualization as a means to *anticipate* future events along with the inherent actions of those events, you *create* opportunity, which is the opportunity to write your own script. As the "director of your own movie" you can be more intentional about the choices you make.

A Quick Visualization Example

Let's choose a random goal of wanting to exercise in the morning prior to starting your day. I know, the thought of sweating immediately upon waking up is enough to send anybody *back* into "nightmare land," but don't worry—this is just hypothetical.

Here's the scenario. Your alarm clock annoyingly buzzes at 6am. Being the mere mortal that you are, the last thing you're going to do is run downstairs, put on your running shoes, and hit the pavement. No, that would suck. After all, you're still rubbing the "sleepies" out of your eyes at this point so you want time to wake up, have a cup of "morning magic" (coffee, as I like to call it) and get in the mindset of sweat. Your goal is to be working out an hour after waking up, so you imagine 7am rolling around and see yourself dropping whatever it is you're doing and heading to the gym.

That's visualization. The key is consistency with the mental cues you use because those cues serve as anchors, which we already discussed. Some practitioners refer to this as If-Then Planning, meaning, that If [insert stimulus here], then [this response occurs].

The psycho-babble version of If-Then planning is *implementation intention*, which is the technical way of referring to doing what you set out to do.

But, implementation doesn't happen without a plan, and that's the intent of If-Then planning.

Psychologist Peter Gollwitzer created this concept in the mid 90's, when he asked his students to mail in an assignment two days before Christmas. One group was simply given the assignment while the other was asked to form specific if-then statements, such as:

- When would they mail it
- Where would they mail it?
- How would they mail it?

The results?

The first group (with no specific instructions) had a 32 percent success rate, whereas the second group who used if-then instructions had a 72 percent success rate[4]. The success rate more than doubled simply by creating a very simple plan; a plan that allowed participants to envision the action they would take when [x] occurred.

Here are some other if-then planning ideas for managing the impulse to "dive-in" to something when you would rather "swim away:"

- If I go to the mall, then I will avoid the book store.
- If I end up in the book store, then I will not buy anything.
- If I go to Amazon, then I will only buy one book.
- If I go out on Friday, then I will only have one drink an hour.
- If I am shopping for Christmas presents, then I will stick to my budget of $x.xx.

See how this works? You envision the stressor (i.e. the mall, the book store, etc…) and you imagine your response to it such that when you're actually there in that position, you've already recited how you will respond so you just "do;" you execute on auto-pilot and save your "thinking" and "willpower" energy for another time.[5]

22. Draw a different conclusion.

No seriously, *draw* it. Rather, draw a decision tree that highlights the following:

Data/information. What do you perceive to accurate? What are your observations about X?

Knowledge. What do you *know* about X? What do you know about the information *about* X? Is it reliable? Accurate?

Experience. What feeling does X generate for you? What might be the opposite feeling and how can that be generated?

Judgment. Why does that feeling exist? Why do you hold your experience to be true? What would discount it?

[5] For an in depth guide to if-then planning as well as mental performance, please visit our Focus Course at www.chaosadvantage.com

Decision making. What will you choose to act upon? To commit to?

Action. When will you act?

Let's assume you want to shift your mindset when it comes to exercise. Specifically, you want to workout early in the morning because you know yourself well enough to realize that the longer the day goes on, the likelihood of working out slowly fades away. This is **information**—knowledge about yourself that you *know* to be true. Hell, you even have data in the form of a habit to show for it (if you're a <u>real</u> numbers person): just tally up how many times you've *wanted* to workout against how many times you *actually* worked out.

However, that's one side of the information coin. This information is also negative in nature because it's self-defeating since the very thought of getting up at the sound of your alarm clock probably makes your eyes roll into the back of your head.

The flipside is this: look at that perspective in a positive light. What's positive about getting up at 6am to go for a run? Absolutely nothing. Just kidding. The positive aspect is that it gives you energy for the day, you've prioritized what's important to you so you begin the day fulfilled, and it sparks your brain to "get in gear" for the day. So, now we have two interpretations of the same coin (see diagram).

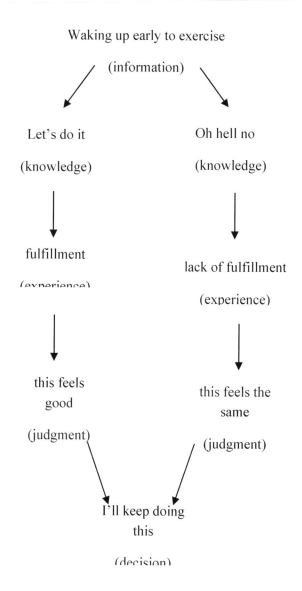

Waking up early to exercise

(information)

Let's do it

(knowledge)

Oh hell no

(knowledge)

fulfillment

(experience)

lack of fulfillment

(experience)

this feels
good

(judgment)

this feels the
same

(judgment)

I'll keep doing
this

(decision)

23. Talk to yourself.

Words have meaning, which gives them power. They impact others and they impact us. Specifically, they impact how we feel about ourselves. Examples of powerful thoughts were given in an earlier chapter so I won't revisit them here, but what I do want to offer is a different perspective on word choice. Let's take a look at two different ways to frame the same sentence.

Sentence #1: "I *have* to workout."

Sentence #2: "I *get* to workout."

What's different about the above sentences? If you gathered that the second sentence infers gratitude, you're right. Sentence #1 implies *force*, pressure to conform, whereas sentence #2 indicates personal choice; a privilege that not everyone has. Here are some other examples:

I don't *have* to visit my friend, I *get* to visit him. It's such privilege to know the value of friendship.

I don't *have* to eat breakfast, I *get* to eat breakfast. I'm so lucky to live in a place where food is abundant.

I don't *have* to go to this meeting, I *get* to go to this meeting. What a privilege to be able to collaborate with diverse and talented people.

You get the idea. This isn't some touchy-feely way of living. Quite the contrary. It's a shift in perspective to focus on the benefit rather than the challenge.

Try this for a week and notice the difference in how you feel. It's very powerful the ability to change our socio-physical state simply through the power of words.

CHAPTER 9

THE SECRET TO BUILDING MENTAL FORTITUDE

BUD/S (Basic Underwater Demolition SEAL Training) is 26 weeks long and divided into three phases: physical conditioning, diving, and land warfare. There are plenty of books out there that will dissect SEAL training with more entertaining stories than what's in this book, so if it's entertainment you seek then I encourage you to put this book down. I also encourage you to ask yourself, "What do I *really* want out of reading this?" If it's a hint of insight coupled with practical exercises to take your mental game to the next level and make you a better performer then please stick around. You've come to the right place after all.

The Secret To Making It Through BUD/S

"The secret to getting through BUD/S is *knowing* you're going to make it through BUD/S." This was the advice one of our instructors gave our class before we entered Hell Week. For the uninitiated, Hell Week is five and a half days of constant, nonstop activity. You're cold, wet, tired, and miserable for 120 hours, sleeping only four hours the entire week.

Yes, it sucks.

However, it's also an INCREDIBLE opportunity to learn about oneself.

After/if you make it through Hell Week you've reached a new subset of people; people who *know* that nothing's impossible; that the only impediment to success is personal volition and that failure is only determined by when and where you choose to stop.

At the same time, Hell Week doesn't instill anything in anybody; it doesn't "make" you anymore mentally tough than before, it just unearths the mental toughness that already existed below the surface by creating the right environment for motivation to flourish and apply one's own mental game.

What does this mean for you?

It means that when we revisit the secret to making it through BUD/S, the same is true for all of us: self-confidence is a mental toughness game changer. Let me explain.

People often attribute mental toughness to one's profession. It's easy for others to say, "Well of course you can do [insert task here], you're a SEAL!" But you know what? Prior to becoming a SEAL, I wasn't. In other words, BUD/S didn't *give* me anything I didn't already have; it just gave me the problem set in which I *chose* to turn the key and unlock my mental toolbox.

"The secret to making it through BUD/S is knowing you're going to make it through BUD/S."

The secret to doing anything, is knowing yourself and knowing you're going to do it.

The Mental Toughness Game Changer

If you *know* deep down in your heart, that there is <u>nothing</u> you can't do, what would stop you?

The answer is nothing.

Nothing would stop you because you <u>believe</u> you can (your *will*), and you believe you can because you possess the competence (your *skill*) to do so. Out of competence and volition emerges self-confidence. After all, can you think of anything that you're passionate about, competent in, but aren't confident enough to execute? Didn't think so.

The takeaway here is this: when you know you can do something (i.e. have the self-confidence) there's nothing you're afraid to pursue.

Intention is the foundation for mental toughness.

A Note On Self-Confidence

If self-confidence is something you want to optimize, here are some practical ways to do so…

1. **Just say "no."** You don't have to assume every responsibility or task that people ask of you, and their feelings won't get hurt if you refuse. After all, you're refusing the task, not the person. I stress this because it's something I see often in executive coaching where managing conflict is a common request amongst clients; they worry that others will see them as unwilling or incompetent if they refuse a project.

But it's just the opposite. If they accept it among the myriad other projects they're working on, then chances are they'll be 60 percent effective for all of them rather than 90 to 95 percent effective had they been more narrowly focused.

2. **Keep your gaze.** When walking by strangers who seem to have never received the memo that staring is rude, maintain your gaze until they look away. Is this contradictory in itself? Yes, but it'll boost your self-confidence I promise. If they don't look away, throw out a healthy, "Hey! How are you?" to quell any nerves.

3. **Assume a power pose.** Amy Cuddy is a social psychologist, Harvard professor, and researcher on nonverbal behavior and snap judgments people make. In her famous TED talk, Amy reveals that we can change not only how we think and feel about ourselves but others' perceptions about us too, simply by engaging in power poses.

"…our bodies change our minds and our minds can change our behavior, and our behavior can change our outcomes." - Amy Cuddy

In a study that used gambling to determine the impact of power posing upon risk tolerance, one group of subjects was told to hold a power pose for two minutes while another group was told to do nothing. The group who assumed the power pose

was 86 percent more likely to gamble compared to just 60 percent of those who did nothing.

The lesson: Practice a power pose for two minutes prior to your next "nervous" event.

4. Speak with confidence. I wrote an article for Forbes[6] one time highlighting the importance of word choice for a leader's effectiveness. Here's the gist of it:

I remember reading a WSJ article one time that talked about grammar snobs in the online dating world and how misspelled words significantly

[6] http://www.forbes.com/sites/jeffboss/

dissuaded potential suitors.

Specifically, match.com polled five thousand singles and asked them what they found to be the number one unattractive quality in a potential partner's profile. Next to hygiene (come on, nobody's going to date you if you smell), it was poor grammar.

Eighty-eight percent of women found misspellings to be a no-go compared to 75 percent of men (I wonder what was important to the men—that's a joke).

Why is this important? Because it's a reflection of character. The words you choose and how you employ them determine how you're received—positively, negatively, influentially or not. Words have powerful implications for not only leaders but everybody surrounding those leaders.

To ensure your message lands on the right runway, follow this guide to choosing the right words:

- **Avoid using contractions**. Words such as "can't," "won't," "shouldn't" are all based off a negative. For instance, replace the statement, "we can't hit these numbers without…" with, "We can hit these numbers when…" Also, notice the avoidance of "if" in the latter sentence. "We can hit these numbers if…" would connote the possibility of failure or choice, but "when" indicates the expectation to execute and fulfill.

- **Replace "try" with "do."** Let me ask this: do you say to your spouse or child, "I love you" or "I'm going to try to love you?" Hopefully it's the former. Words like "try," "want" (i.e. "I want to…[insert 'but' here]" connote a lack of commitment, of uncertainty.

- **Use words that influence**. Using words such as "just," "kind of," "sort of," "a little," "maybe," "I think," and "some" all have less impact than their assertive counterparts, so replace "I think" with "I believe." Again, do or do not, there is no try.

- **Communicate choice rather than compulsion**. The phrase "I have to…" conveys a lack of personal choice, as if an external influence is forcing you to do something. The same goes for "I need to." Choice indicates confidence and purpose. Replace "I have to" with "I want to" or "I will" if you want to sound more assertive.

- **Avoid "probably" at all costs**. There's
  nothing worse than a leader who is unsure of
  him or herself but afraid to admit it, and the
  word "probably" infers just that—a 50
  percent chance of success and a 50 percent
  chance of failure. Does that make any sense?
  It shouldn't. If you're unsure of something
  the best thing to do is just say so. Honesty
  and transparency go a long way. Remember,
  the best way to build trust is to begin trusting.

- **Choose common words**. One of my favorite
  sayings is this: nobody cares how much you
  know, until they know how much you care.
  Choose words that an eighth grader would
  understand for two reasons. First, it
  humanizes you. Excessively long or
  uncommon words communicate one thing:
  "I'm smarter than you and I'm going to use
  'smart' words to prove it." Second, insecurity
  is easily discernible through vocabulary, and
  smart people see right through "big words."
  There's no need to use a fifty-dollar
  word when a single dollar will suffice. Don't
  get me wrong, an extensive vocabulary is
  important. All I'm saying is be mindful

of when, where, why and with whom you employ the big ones. Save the big guns for the "big guns."

Choose your words wisely to optimize your mental game.

However, what I didn't mention in the above was the importance of tone and volume. *How* a message is delivered is oftentimes more effective than *what* is delivered.

5. Pause before saying "um." If you feel an "um" or an "uh" approaching, take a momentary pause to collect your thoughts, then speak. It's that simple.

6. Set—and accomplish—goals. The difference between a goal and a to-do list is goals challenge you to grow; to-do lists don't. The feeling of accomplishment gleaned from realizing a goal provides greater confidence in setting and achieving larger ones. Research suggests that we tend to regret that which we haven't done more than what we've already accomplished. The most important benefit of goal-setting when it comes to building self-confidence is that it forges you as the type of person *to* achieve goals. That in and of itself is a significant confidence booster. Make yourself a small goal right now and commit to achieving it. It might be waking up early, avoiding that sugary drink or having that conversation you've been avoiding for so long. Whatever it is, make it happen. I promise you'll feel a newfound sense of self-confidence.

Chapter 10
10 INGREDIENTS OF MENTAL FORTITUDE

I was once asked the difference between discipline and grit, and my answer was this: Discipline helps you "get through" a workout; grit "propels" you through it. If you were to compare the 175ish students who started in my BUD/S class (SEAL training) with the 34 of us who finished, I'd say that one of the distinguishing factors was grit.

Discipline directs, but grit decides. What I mean is, those students who made it up to Hell Week (a significant selector of BUD/S graduates) were certainly disciplined. They woke up every day for training, they participated in every training evolution, and they were cold, wet, tired and miserable just like the rest of us—right up until the point they quit.

You see, it's not that these students weren't disciplined, simply that they chose not to exercise a choice that others did. That choice was to continue on, and *that* is grit.

Grit was one thing that separated the successful students from the failed.

Angela Duckworth, assistant professor Angela Duckworth of the University of Pennsylvania, in infamous TED talk highlighted that "when it comes to high achievement, grit may be as essential as intelligence."

Specifically, grit is "a passionate commitment to a single mission and an unswerving dedication to achieve that

> It has been said that 80percent of success in life is just showing up. Grit is one thing that determines who shows up.

mission." What this looks like is:

- consistency of passion

- consistency of effort

- single-minded approach toward goals

- obsession with certain activities

Additional research by Dennis Charney of the Icahn School of Medicine at Mount Sinai in New York City and Steven Southwick of the Yale School of Medicine highlight ten factors that allow the most resilient among us to keep going despite incredibly trying times:

Facing fear

Having a moral compass

Drawing on faith

Using social support

Having good role models

Being physically fit

Making sure your brain is challenged

Having "cognitive and emotional flexibility"

Having "meaning, purpose, and growth" in life

"Realistic" optimism

How do you develop these factors? Deliberate practice—and that starts with focus.

<u>Exercise: Focus</u>

1.   Set a timer for 45 seconds

2.   Focus your attention on one thought. It can be anything, such as a recent movie, your neighbor, your favorite pair of shoes…

3.   Focus your full attention on this one thing and <u>nothing else.</u>

4.   Do not pay attention to any other thoughts or sounds until the time is up.

Ready? Go.

So, how'd it go? Were you able to maintain focus? Or, did a random thought pop into your head? If you're like the majority of people, then your mind probably wandered.

Hey, it's normal.

But, here's why it's so important to be able to harness the mind's propensity to drift: the mind will wander 46.9 percent of the time, according to research in the book One Second Ahead: Enhance Your Performance At Work With Mindfulness.

In other words, only 53.1 percent of the time we spend at work is actually focused on a particular task. The rest of the time, who knows what it's focused on? The key to focusing on anything is to be absorbed in the moment; to be "present" such that nothing else enters your mind and all you focus on is that one particular task.

CONCLUSION

Fear, uncertainty, and chance can all seem impenetrable. After all, how do you know you'll be good at something if you've never done it? However, another way to look at it is this: How do you know that you won't?

Mental fortitude is fundamental to optimal performance—in anything.

There was a saying in BUD/S that went, "Lead with the mind and the body will follow," and I've found that to be completely true.

It takes consistent, deliberate practice to apply the exercises and thought processes outlined in this book, and I'm not going to lie, none of this stuff is easy. But then again, chances are you wouldn't have bought this book if "easy" defined you.

If you'd like one-on-one coaching to bring your performance to the next level, please contact me at my website www.chaosadvantage.com.

References

For a complete list of references, please visit
www.chaosadvantage.com

Navigating Chaos: How To Find Certainty In Uncertain Situations

Available at Amazon, Barnes & Noble, and iTunes

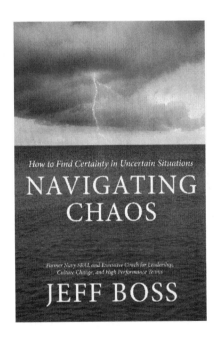

ABOUT THE AUTHOR

Jeff Boss is co-founder of Chaos Advantage,
a professionally certified executive and team coach, author,
weekly contributor to Forbes and Entrepreneur, co-founder
of the Adaptability Metric, founding team member of the
SEAL Future Fund, and former Navy SEAL who is fueled by
sarcasm, scotch, and all good things. Visit him online at
http://www.chaosadvantage.com/

Made in the USA
Middletown, DE
01 October 2017